T-SHIRT GRAPHICS

NEW YORK LONDON TOKYO LOS ANGELES
SAN FRANCISCO OSAKA DALLAS AMSTERDAM BOSTON
PARIS SYDNEY FERRARA DALLAS ATLANTA MILANO SEATTLE MIAMI
HONG KONG

P·I·E BOOKS

T-SHIRT GRAPHICS

Copyright © 1992 by P·I·E BOOKS

All right reserved.
No part of this work may be reproduced in
any form without written permission of
the publisher.

Firtst published in Japan in 1992 by :
P·I·E BOOKS
Villa Phoenix Suite 407, 4-14-6, Komagome,
Toshima-ku, Tokyo 170, JAPAN
TEL 03-3949-5010 FAX 03-3949-5650
ISBN 4-938586-33-9 C3070 P16000E

First Published in Germany in 1992 by:
NIPPAN
NIppon Shuppan Hanbai Deutschland GmbH
Krefelder Str.85 D-4000 Düsseldert 11(Heerdt)
TEL 0211 5048089 FAX 0211 5049326

ISBN 3-910052-18-5

Printed in Japan

PREFACE 5

FASHION 8

SPORTS 108

CREATIVE SERVICES 142

CONTENTS

MUSIC 155

EVENTS 171

ORGANIZATIONS 188

MISCELLANEOUS 200

SUBMITORS' INDEX 219

EDITORIAL NOTE:

CD: Creative Director
AD: Art Director
D: Designer
P: Photographer
I: Illustrator
PR: Producer
PL: Planner
DF: Design Firm
I/R: Importer/Retailer
CL: Client

序

　本書はロンドン、ニューヨーク、ロサンジェルス、東京等を中心に世界各地から寄せられた2000着以上のTシャツのなかからデザイン的に優れた約700作品を紹介している。

　ファッションメーカー、スポーツメーカーは消費者の多様化するニーズに合わせて、毎年実に多種多用なデザインのTシャツを発表している。他のファッションアイテムと比較してTシャツはコストが安いためデザインのバリエーションを増やし制作することが可能であり、ヴィジュアルとしてデザイナーが最も自分のセンスを表現できるアイテムでもある。

　また一般企業や団体等はCIのアプリケーションやセールスプロモーションのためにTシャツを制作する機会が多い。中でもイベントの際には必ずといっていいほどTシャツは制作されている。スタッフのユニフォームとして、あるいは記念として配付されたりしている。

　このようにTシャツが数多く制作されているのはTシャツにしかない魅力があるからである。例えばコンピュータグラフィックスを用い、本来はグラフィックスのためにデザインされたものがCOTTON100％の生地にプリントされるとまた別の魅力をもってしまう。デザインが身近な存在となり、デザインを楽しんで"見る"だけのものではなく"着る"ものに変化するからでもある。様々なデザインの中から自分の気に入ったものを選び出し、"着る"という行為自体が魅力なのではないだろうか。なかには珍しい貴重なTシャツを求めて世界を駆け巡っている人もいるという話がある。またデザインする側にとっては着てもらう楽しさ、デザインに共感してもらう喜びがある。

　Tシャツはデザインを楽しむものであるがメディアとしてメッセージTシャツの存在を忘れてはいけない。今回、ロサンジェルスのスタッフが取材をしている際に不幸にも暴動事件が発生した。取材の作業は遅れはしたが、しばらくしてスタッフからロサンジェルス暴動に対するメッセージのTシャツが届けられた。暴動が発生して間もないのにすでにTシャツは制作されていたのである。人種差別、平和問題、動物保護、エイズ問題等様々な人類の諸問題に対してメッセージを投げかけるメッセージTシャツ。そういったメッセージTシャツを着るという行為は自分の意見を表明しているということである。本書でも何点かそのようなメッセージTシャツを紹介しているが、その中にはデザイン的に優れたものがあり、Tシャツをデザインするデザイナーがメッセージに対して共感する、あるいは伝えたいという真摯な姿勢がデザインに現われているのではないだろうか。

　新しいタイプのものとしてサイクリング関係のものについていえば、いわゆるTシャツという概念とは多少違いはあるが、そのポップな色使いやデザインはスポーツウェアという機能性を重視した上で実にデザインレベルの高いものである。本書のタイトルをT-shirt Graphicsとしているためジャージ素材のサイクリングシャツを掲載してよいのか迷いはしたが、このような優れたデザインを他では紹介する機会が少ないので本書では紹介させていただいた。木を見て森を見ないということを避けたかったからである。世界中の優れたグラフィックスを紹介するというのが私達グラフィック書を出版する会社の使命であり目的でもある。たった一つの言葉に捕われ、その本質を見失うようなことはしたくなかったからである。同様にトレーナー、パーカー等についても本書では紹介することにした。

　最後に、この書籍に快く協力してくれた皆様に感謝いたします。

ピエ ブックス

PREFACE

This book Showcases 700 outstanding T-shirts which were selected from more than 2000 submissions sent in from all over the world including such major centers as London, Los Angeles, New york and Tokyo.

Fashion makers and sporting-goods makers put out a great variety of T-shirt designs every year to cater to the ever diversifying desires of contemporary consumers. Because T-shirts are relatively inexpensive to manufacture, compared to other fashion items, it is possible to produce them in a wider variety of designs. Hence, T-shirts turn out to be a most responsive and visual medium for designers who wish express their fashion sensibilities.

Businesses and organizations that have nothing to do with the fashion industry often have T-shirts produced for corporate identity, as PR material for sales promotions and special events. Often these T-shirts are worn by staffers as uniforms at such events, distributed as souvenirs or may end-up being distributed commercially.

For a variety of reasons, vast numbers of T-shirts are being produced every year and they do have their own inimitable charm. For example, when a computer-generated image or a design which was originally intended as graphic art is printed on 100% cotton fabric, the image is given a whole new life. It brings the artwork closer to the people since it is no longer just an abstract design to be looked at. Now it has become something more personal; something you actually put on. The great attraction of T-shirts is in being able to choose something you really like from a myriad of available designs and wear it as a personal statement. We hear of people who travel all over the world looking for rare, original T-shirts which no body else will be seen wearing.

For the designer, having people walking around with his designs on their chest or back is a special joy. What more genuine gesture of appreciation could there be than to buy and wear a design on your body?

T-shirts are fundamentally something people should enjoy for the sheer pleasure of good visual design. However, message T-shirts, as a form of communication media have a serious side. During the production of this book, for example, the rioting which followed the Rodney King incident in L.A. occurred while our staff was in that city collecting material. Within a matter of days we received our first T-shirt with a message about the riots. Such T-shirts were designed, manufactured and put into circulation before the event had even run its course. We wondered what other media could respond to current events so rapidly.

The act of putting on a message T-shirt is equivalent to airing your opinion on the issues of your choice. People can publicly comment on racial discrimination, the armed forces, environmental protection, AIDS or any other major issue we face today, by donning a T-shirt. In this book we have included several of these message T-shirts, selected on the basis of their outstanding graphic quality. We have to suppose that the designers who created these graphics must agree wholeheartedly with their message and that the excellence of the design is, in part, a reflection of their passion to convey the message.

I would like to refer to the cycling-related items included here. They do not exactly fit the usual definition of a T-shirt, but the way designers are using POP colors and bold graphic elements is a new and exciting development in sports gear, where the importance has traditionally been on functionality. We felt, at first, a little hesitate about including cycling jerseys, since the title of this book was to be "T-shirt Graphics." There are not many opportunities, however, to showcase the kind of great designs we found among them, so we decided to carry them despite the questionable semantics. After all, our purpose here has more to do with graphic design than apparel and we wanted to bring you the very best of what we could find. So we decided to introduce some trainers and parkas in the book as well.

Before we leave you, we would like to express our sincere appreciation of all the people who have been so cooperative in the production of this book.

P·I·E BOOKS

VORWORT

Dieses Buch präsentiert 700 herausragende T-Shirts, ausgewählt aus über 2000 Designs aus aller Welt, einschließlich solch wichtiger Modezentren wie London, Los Angeles, New York und Tokyo.

Mode- und Sportartikel-Hersteller produzieren jedes Jahr eine Vielfalt von T-Shirts, um dem sich ständig wandelnden Geschmack der modernen Kunden gerecht zu werden. Da T-Shirts im Vergleich zu anderen Modetextilien relativ preiswert herzustellen sind, kann eine große Bandbreite von Designs angeboten werden. Für Designer, die ihr Mode-Feeling rapide ausdrücken wollen, sind T-Shirts ein dankbares Objekt.

Auch solche Firmen und Organisationen, die nichts mit der Mode-Industrie zu tun haben, lassen sich häufig T-Shirts für Corporate Identity-, für PR- und für Sales Promotion-Zwecke herstellen. Oft werden diese T-Shirts auch von Firmenangehörigen zu besonderen Anlässen getragen, als Souvenirs verteilt oder gar verkauft.

Aus den verschiedensten Gründen werden Jahr für Jahr Massen von T-Shirts hergestellt - und alle haben ihren eigenen Reiz. Wenn zum Beispiel ein computer-generiertes Bild oder Design, das ursprünglich für einen anderen Grafik-Design-Zweck entworfen wurde, auf 100% Baumwolle gedruckt wird, gibt das dem Bild ein völlig neues Leben. Es bringt das Image näher zu dem Menschen, es ist nicht mehr länger ein abstraktes Design zum Anschauen. Nun ist es etwas persönliches, etwas, das man tragen kann. Die große Attraktion der T-Shirts liegt nicht zuletzt darin, daß man sich etwas nach seinem persönlichen Geschmack aus einer riesigen Menge von Designs aussuchen kann und es dann auch als Ausdruck seiner eigenen Persönlichkeit tragen kann. Man hört soger von Leuten, die von kaum jemandem getragene, rare Original-T-Shirts aus aller Welt sammeln.

Für jeden T-Shirt-Designer ist es eine spezielle Freude, Leute mit dem eigenen Design auf Brust oder Rücken herumlaufen zu sehen. Was könnte es für eine direktere Geste der Wertschätzung eines Designs geben, als es zu kaufen und am eigenen Körper zu tragen?

T-Shirts sind grundsätzlich etwas, an dem sich Leute nur wegen des guten visuellen Designs erfreuen können. T-Shirts als eine Form eines Kommunikationsmittels mit aufgedruckten Botschaften haben jedoch auch eine ernste Seite. Während der Produktion dieses Buches, zum Beispiel, als unsere Mitarbeiter noch Bildmaterial sammelten, ereigneten sich in Los Angeles die schweren Unruhen. Innerhalb nur weniger Tage erhielten wir unser erstes T-Shirt mit einer Aussage über den Aufstand. Solche T-Shirts wurden entworfen, produziert und in Umlauf gebracht, bevor noch die Ereignisse zu Ende waren. Erstaunlich für uns, wie schnell dieses Medium auf laufende Ereignisse reagieren kann.

Ein T-Shirt mit einer Botschaft anzuziehen ist gleichzusetzen damit, diese Botschaft laut zu äußern. Leute kommentieren so in aller Öffentlichkeit über Rassendiskriminierung, die Armee, über Umweltschutz, AIDS und andere wichtige Probleme unserer Zeit. In diesem Buch zeigen wir eine Reihe dieser »Message T-Shirts«, ausgewählt wegen ihrer herausragenden graphischen Qualität. Wir haben unterstellt, daß die Designer dieser Graphiken von ganzem Herzen hinter der Botschaft stehen. Folgerichtig ist die Qualität des Designs ein Spiegelbild der Leidenschaft, die jeweilige Botschaft zu vermitteln.

Noch ein Wort zu den Trikots aus dem Fahrradbereich in diesem Buch. Sie entsprechen nicht exakt der gewöhnlichen Definition eines T-Shirts. Aber die Art, in der Designer Pop-Farben und kräftige Graphik-Elemente benutzen, ist eine neue, aufregende Entwicklung in der Sportbekleidung. Eigentlich kommt es dort eher auf Funktionalität an. Zunächst haben wir etwas gezögert, die Fahrrad-Trikots in diesem Buch »T-Shirt Graphics« vorzustellen. Da es allerdings kaum eine andere Gelegenheit gibt, diese großartigen Designs zu präsentieren, haben wir uns entschlossen, sie in das Buch aufzunehmen. Ist es doch vorrangiger Zweck dieses Buches, gelungenes Graphik-Design zu präsentieren. Aus diesem Grunde haben wir auch das Beste, was wir an Parkas und Trainingsbekleidung fanden, in das Buch aufgenommen.

Zum Schluß möchten wir uns bei allen recht herzlich bedanken, die uns bei der Produktion dieses Buches geholfen haben.

P·I·E BOOKS

FRONT BACK

BODY RAP ▲
UK 1991
P:Industria

▼ **BODY RAP**
UK 1992
P:Stephen Klein

FRONT BACK

LOS ANGELES HONG KONG BOSTON PARIS

BODY RAP
UK 1992
P:Stephen Klein

BODY RAP
UK 1992
P:Tracey Collins

BODY RAP
UK 1991
P:Industria

BODY RAP
UK 1992
P:Herb Ritts

AMSTERDAM 011 PHILADELPHIA LONDON

RARA TOKYO SEATTLE HELSINKI MIAMI LOS

BODY RAP
UK 1991
P:Industria

BODY RAP
UK 1990
P:Pierre & Gilles

BODY RAP
UK 1992
P:Dougie Fields

BODY RAP
UK 1992
P:Dougie Fields

CO OSAKA NEW YORK 012 MILANO DALLAS A

GELES HONG KONG BOSTON PARIS SAN FRAN

FRONT BACK

BODY RAP ▲
UK 1991
P:Enrique Badulescu

▼ **BODY RAP**
UK 1991
P:Enrique Badulescu

FRONT BACK

TERDAM PHILADELPHIA LONDON 013 SYDNE

KYO SEATTLE HELSINKI MIAMI LOS ANGELES

BODY RAP
UK 1992
D:Me Company

BODY RAP
UK 1992
D:Me Company

BODY RAP
UK 1991
P:Herb Ritts

BODY RAP
UK 1992
P:Herb Ritts

EW YORK MILANO DALLAS 014 AMSTERDAM

NG KONG BOSTON PARIS SAN FRANCISCO OS

KEN BROWN
USA 1991
I:Ken Brown DF:Ken Brown Designs

KEN BROWN
USA 1985
I:Ken Brown DF:Ken Brown Designs

KEN BROWN
USA 1991
I:Ken Brown DF:Ken Brown Designs

D.BROOKS
USA 1989
D:David Brooks DF:D.Brooks Design

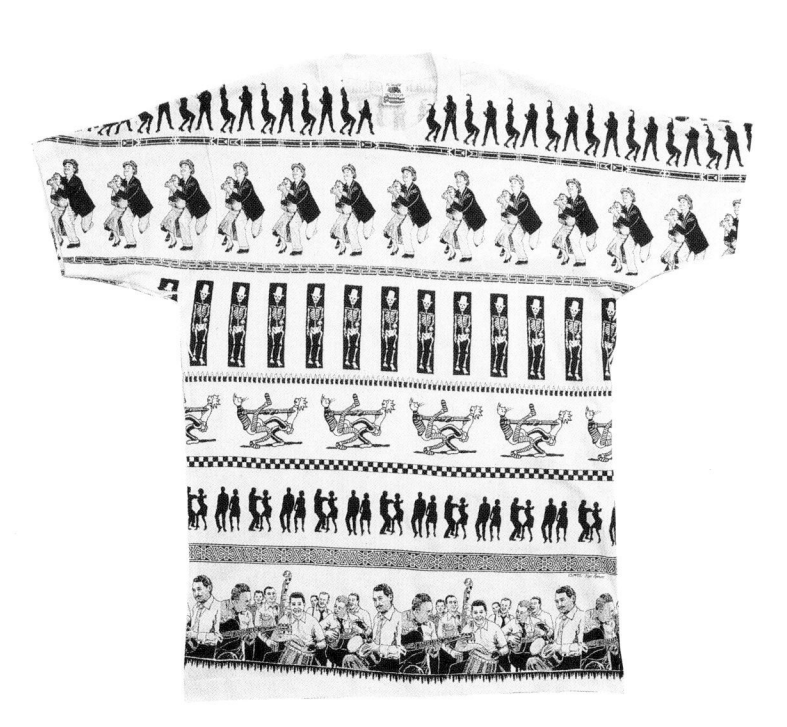

ILADELPHIA LONDON SYDNEY 015 ATLANTA

KEN BROWN
USA 1990
I:Ken Brown DF:Ken Brown Designs

KEN BROWN
USA 1990
I:Ken Brown DF:Ken Brown Designs

KEN BROWN
USA 1991
I:Ken Brown DF:Ken Brown Designs

KEN BROWN
USA 1991
D,I:Ken Brown DF:Ken Brown Designs

G BOSTON PARIS SAN FRANCISCO OSAKA NE

D.BROOKS
USA 1990
D:David Brooks DF:D.Brooks Design

.PHIA LONDON 017 SYDNEY ATLANTA FERRA

FRONT

OZONE COMMUNITY
JAPAN 1989
CL:Ozone Community Co.,Ltd.

BACK

TON PARIS SAN FRANCISCO OSAKA NEW YOR

OZONE COMMUNITY ▲
JAPAN 1989
CL:Ozone Community Co.,Ltd.

▼ **OZONE COMMUNITY**
JAPAN 1989
CL:Ozone Community Co.,Ltd.

LONDON SYDNEY ATLANTA 019 FERRARA TO

MIAMI LOS ANGELES HONG KONG BOSTON P

BODY RAP
UK 1992
P:Pierre & Gilles

BODY RAP
UK 1992
P:Pierre & Gilles

BUNKAYA ZAKKATEN
THAILAND 1992
I/R:Bunkaya Zakkaten

BODY RAP
UK 1992
P:Pierre & Gilles

AS 020 AMSTERDAM PHILADELPHIA LONDO

IS SAN FRANCISCO OSAKA NEW YORK MILAN

D.BROOKS
USA 1986
D,I:David Brooks DF:D.Brooks Design

D.BROOKS
USA 1990
D:David Brooks DF:D.Brooks Design

GURTLER+HAZELL
UK 1991
D:Guy Hazell DF:Gurtler+Hazell

ARCHAIC SMILE
USA 1992
D:Rachel-Jeff

SYDNEY 021 ATLANTA FERRARA TOKYO SEAT

LOS ANGELES HONG KONG BOSTON PARIS SA

ARCHAIC SMILE
USA 1991
D:Rachel-Jeff

ARCHAIC SMILE
USA 1991
D:Rachel-Jeff

OZONE COMMUNITY
JAPAN 1992
CL:Ozone Community Co.,Ltd.

RNA
JAPAN 1992
CL:RNA Inc.

STERDAM PHILADELPHIA 022 LONDON SYDN

FRANCISCO OSAKA NEW YORK MILANO DALL

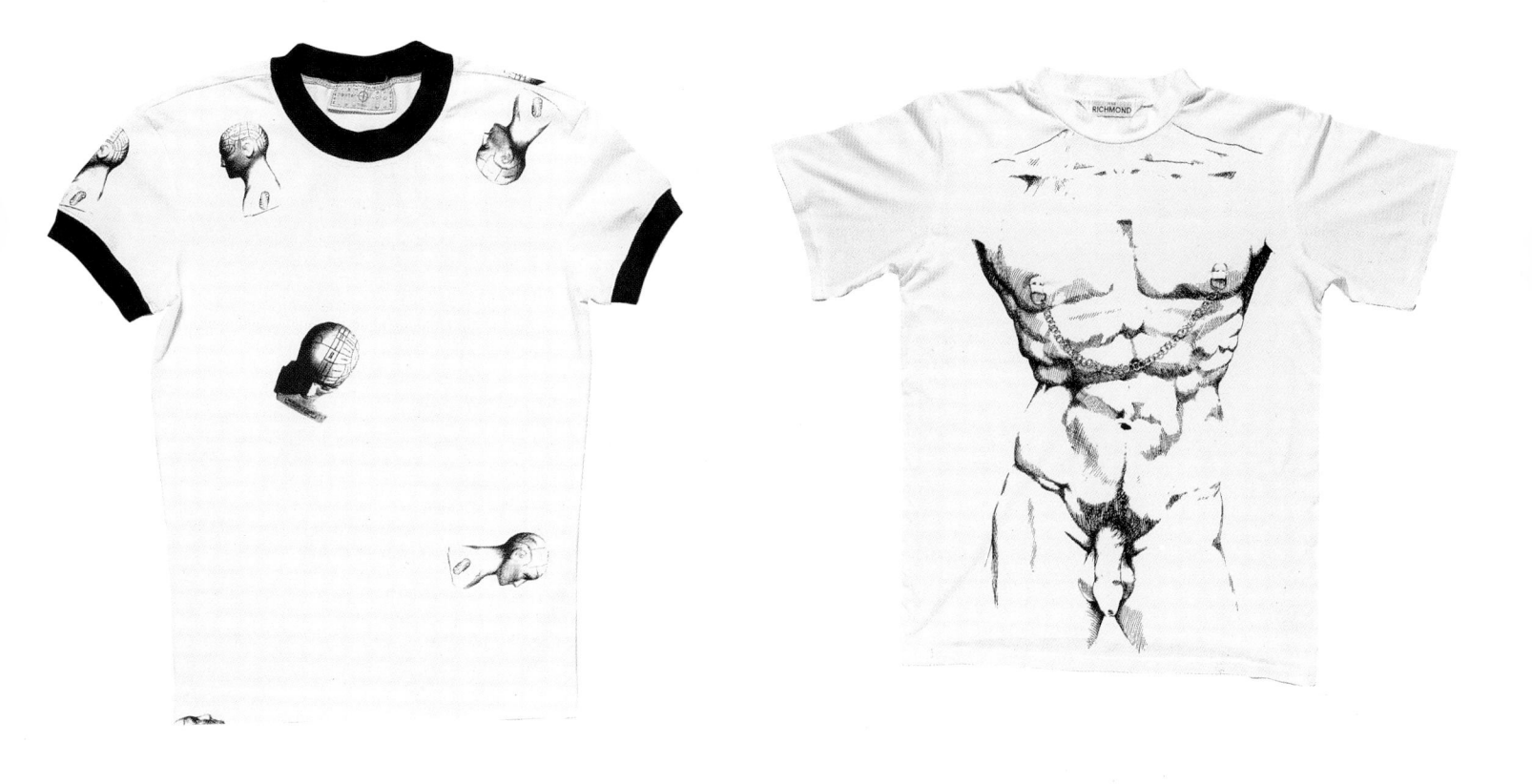

DEXTER WONG
UK 1992
D:Dexter Wong

JOHN RICHMOND
UK 1988
D:John Richmond

ESCHER
USA 1991
D:Los Angeles T-shirt Museum

FRONT

BACK

ATLANTA FERRARA 023 TOKYO SEATTLE HE

ISSEY MIYAKE ▲
JAPAN 1992
AD,D:Tadanori Yokoo DF:Miyake Design Studio
CL:Issey Miyake Co.,Ltd.

▼ **BRONZINO**
UK 1991
D:G & H"After Bronzino" DF:Gurtler+Hazell

SCO OSAKA NEW YORK MILANO DALLAS AMS

ARCHAIC SMILE
USA 1992
D:Rachel-Jeff

TA 025 FERRARA TOKYO SEATTLE HELSINKI

OZONE COMMUNITY
JAPAN 1989
CL:Ozone Community Co.,Ltd.

OZONE COMMUNITY
JAPAN 1988
CL:Ozone Community Co.,Ltd.

OZONE COMMUNITY
JAPAN 1989
CL:Ozone Community Co.,Ltd.

OZONE COMMUNITY
JAPAN 1988
CL:Ozone Community Co.,Ltd.

AKA NEW YORK MILANO DALLAS AMSTERDAM

OZONE COMMUNITY
JAPAN 1990
CL:Ozone Community Co.,Ltd.

BETTY'S BLUE
JAPAN 1992
CL:Lemon Co.,Ltd.

OZONE COMMUNITY
JAPAN 1992
CL:Ozone Community Co.,Ltd.

F·B·I & S·P.CO.
JAPAN 1992
CD:Takahisa Kamiya AD:Etsuro Kusunoki
D:Isao Okochi CL:Super Planning Co.,Ltd.

RARA TOKYO 027 SEATTLE HELSINKI MIAMI

KONG BOSTON PARIS SAN FRANCISCO OSAKA

COLIN HARVEY
UK 1992
D:Colin Harvey

COLIN HARVEY
UK 1992
D:Colin Harvey

COLIN HARVEY
UK 1992
D:Colin Harvey

COLIN HARVEY
UK 1992
D:Colin Harvey

DON SYDNEY ATLANTA 028 FERRARA TOKYO

NEW YORK MILANO DALLAS AMSTERDAM PHI

FRONT

COLIN HARVEY
UK 1992
D:Colin Harvey

BACK

EATTLE HELSINKI MIAMI 029 LOS ANGELS HO

MICHIKO KOSHINO
UK 1992
D:Michiko Koshino

BOYS OWN/GLOBAL GUIDE
UK 1992
D:Philip Goss

JOE CASELY-HAYFORD
UK 1992
D:Joe Casely-Hayford DF:Joe Casely-Hayford

JOE CASELY-HAYFORD
UK 1992
D:Joe Casely-Hayford DF:Joe Casely-Hayford

DALLAS AMSTERDAM PHILADELPHIA LON DO

DEXTER WONG
UK 1992
D:Dexter Wong

DEXTER WONG
UK 1992
D:Dexter Wong

DEXTER WONG
UK 1992
D:Dexter Wong

DEXTER WONG
UK 1992
D:Dexter Wong

TLE HELSINKI 031 MIAMI LOS ANGELES HON

HELTER SKELTER
JAPAN 1992
CL:Big Company

MACROCOSM
JAPAN 1992
D:Naoko Kiyota,Kiyoshi Hazemoto
I/R:Thirty-Three

"X"CLOTHES
UK 1988
D:The Designers Republic
DF:The Designers Republic CL:Street Clothes

"X"CLOTHES
UK 1988
D:The Designers Republic
DF:The Designers Republic CL:Street Clothes

"X"CLOTHES
UK 1988
D:The Designers Republic
DF:The Designers Republic CL:Street Clothes

GURTLER+HAZELL
UK 1992
D:Guy Hazell DF:Gurtler+Hazell

STRANGE ATTRACTIONS
UK 1991
D:Greg Sams DF:Strange Attractions

STRANGE ATTRACTIONS
UK 1991
D:Greg Sams DF:Strange Attractions

STRANGE ATTRACTIONS
UK 1991
D:Greg Sams DF:Strange Attractions

JOHN RICHMOND
UK 1988
D:John Richmond

GURTLER+HAZELL
UK 1992
D:Guy Hazell DF:Gurtler+Hazell

JOHN RICHMOND
UK 1988
D:John Richmond

JOHN RICHMOND
UK 1988
D:John Richmond

SAKA NEW YORK MILANO DALLAS AMSTERD

GRAPHIC MANIPULATOR
JAPAN 1991
D:Sumio Takemoto I/R:Thirty-Three

ISSEY MIYAKE
JAPAN 1991
AD,D,I:Tadanori Yokoo DF:Miyake Design Studio
CL:Issey Miyake Co.,Ltd.

TYCOON
JAPAN 1991
D:Toshio Nakanishi CL:Club King Co.

TYCOON
JAPAN 1991
D:Toshio Nakanishi CL:Club King Co.

A TOKYO 036 SEATTLE HELSINKI MIAMI LOS

PHILADELPHIA LONDON SYDNEY ATLANTA F

TYCOON
JAPAN 1990
D:Toshio Nakanishi CL:Club King Co.

CLUB KING
JAPAN 1991
D:See Gee Gen CL:Club King Co.

JOE BOXER CORP.
USA 1990
D:Nicholas Graham

FLOWERS
JAPAN 1992
CL:Lemon Co.,Ltd.

GELES 037 HONG KONG BOSTON PARIS SAN

SJOBECK
USA 1992
I/R:Nine Too Zero

SJOBECK
USA 1992
I/R:Nine Too Zero

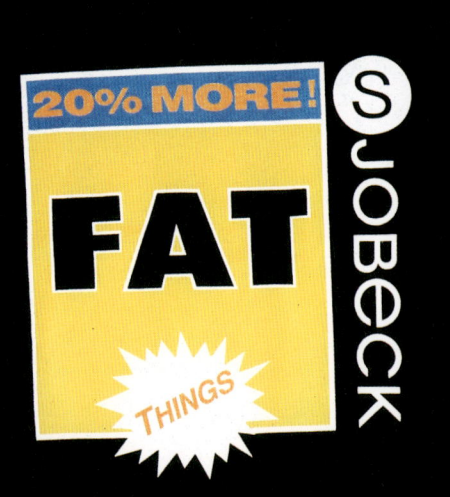

SJOBECK
USA 1992
I/R:Nine Too Zero

FLOWERS
JAPAN 1992
CL:Lemon Co.,Ltd.

SJOBECK
USA 1992
I/R:Nine Too Zero

NINE TOO ZERO
JAPAN 1992
D:Nine Too Zero CL:Nine Too Zero

SJOBECK
USA 1992
I/R:Nine Too Zero

SJOBECK
USA 1992
I/R:Nine Too Zero

BACK

FRONT

TYCOON ▲
JAPAN 1989
D:Toshio Nakanishi CL:Club King Co.

▼ **CAPTAIN PLANET**
JAPAN 1992
CD:Yuji Imanishi D:Patrick Glover
CL:The Planet Plan, Inc.

FRONT

BACK

ON SYDNEY ATLANTA FERRARA TOKYO SEAT

FRONT BACK

CAPTAIN PLANET ▲
JAPAN 1992
CD:Yuji Imanishi D:Patrick Glover
CL:The Planet Plan, Inc.

▼ CLUB KING
JAPAN 1991
D:See Gee Gen CL:Club King Co.

FRONT BACK

STON PARIS 041 SAN FRANCISCO OSAKA N

CLUB KING
JAPAN
D:Wataru Komachi CL:Club King Co.

CLUB KING
JAPAN 1992
D:Club King CL:Club King Co.

CLUB KING
JAPAN 1992
D:Club King CL:Club King Co.

SWIFTY
UK 1992
AD,D:Ian Swift DF:Swifty Typographics
CL:Swifty Favourite Gears

...NEY ATLANTA FERRARA TOKYO SEATTLE HEL

GRAPHIC MANIPULATOR
JAPAN 1991
D:Sumio Takemoto I/R:Thirty-Three

RED OR DEAD
UK 1992
D:Kate Cullinan,Gary Page CL:Red or Dead

JOE CASELY-HAYFORD
UK 1992
D:Joe Casely-Hayford DF:Joe Casely-Hayford

RICHMOND-DESTROY
UK 1991
D:John Richmond

PARIS SAN FRANCISCO OSAKA 043 NEW YOR...

SAB STREET
JAPAN 1992
CL:Aterier Sab Co.,Ltd.

HELTER SKELTER
JAPAN 1992
CL:Big Company

HELTER SKELTER
JAPAN 1992
CL:Big Company

RICHMOND/CORNEJO
UK 1984
D:John Richmond,David Richmond

MEN'S BA-TSU
   JAPAN 1992
   CL:Ba-tsu Co.,Ltd.

JOE BOXER CORP.
   USA 1992
   D:Nicholas Graham

TYCOON
   JAPAN 1989
   D:Toshio Nakanishi CL:Club King Co.

JOE BOXER CORP.
   USA 1988
   D:Nicholas Graham

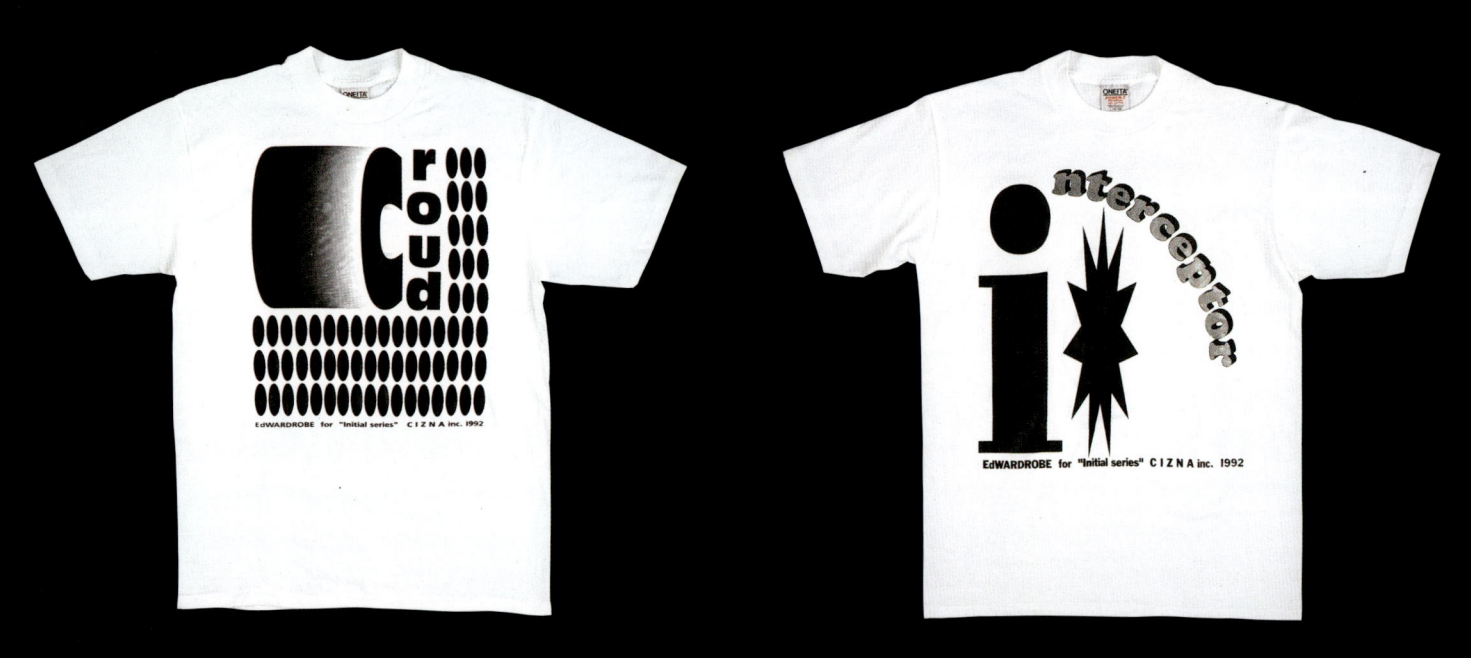

EDWARD
JAPAN 1992
I:Edward Tsuwaki CL:Cizna Inc.

A TOKYO SEATTLE HELSINKI MIAMI LOS ANG

EDWARD
JAPAN 1992
I:Edward Tsuwaki CL:Cizna Inc.

SAKA NEW YORK MILANO 047 DALLAS AMSTE

LONDON SYDNEY ATLANTA FERRARA TOKYO

DOUBLE FACE
USA 1991
D:Kiyoko Yabuki I/R:Thirty-Three

GRAPHIC MANIPULATOR
JAPAN 1991
D:Sumio Takemoto I/R:Thirty-Three

BA-TSU CLUB
JAPAN 1992
CL:Ba-tsu Co.,Ltd.

ABLE INTERNET
JAPAN 1990
D,I:Keiko Habara DF:Atelier Neu!! Inc.
CL:Maruzeniya Co.,Ltd.

DOUBLE FACE ▲
USA 1991
D:Kyoko Yabuki I/R:Thirty-Three

▼ GRAPHIC MANIPULATOR
JAPAN 1992
D:Sumio Takemoto I/R:Thirty-Three

SYDNEY ATLANTA FERRARA TOKYO SEATTL

T·A·R·(TOKYO AIR RUNNERS)
JAPAN 1990
D:Toshiyuki Seki I/R:Thirty-Three

BETTY'S BLUE
JAPAN 1992
CL:Lemon Co.,Ltd.

FLOWERS
JAPAN 1992
CL:Lemon Co.,Ltd.

PERSON'S FOR MEN
JAPAN 1992
CL:Person's Co.,Ltd.

PARIS SAN FRANCISCO 050 OSAKA NEW YO

HELSINKI MIAMI LOS ANGELES HONG KONG

GRAPHIC MANIPULATOR
JAPAN 1992
D:Sumio Takemoto I/R:Thirty-Three

CAPTAIN PLANET
JAPAN 1992
CD:Yuji Imanishi D:Ian Wright
CL:The Planet Plan,Inc.

CAPTAIN PLANET
JAPAN 1992
CD:Yuji Imanishi D:Matt Campbell
CL:The Planet Plan,Inc.

KANSAI O2
JAPAN 1992
D:Kansai Company CL:Kansai Company

MILANO DALLAS 051 AMSTERDAM PHILADE

ATLANTA FERRARA TOKYO SEATTLE HELSIN

FRONT　　　　　　　　　　　　　　　BACK

CAPTAIN PLANET ▲
JAPAN 1992
CD:Yuji Imanishi D:Patrick Glover
CL:The Planet Plan,Inc.

▼ CAPTAIN PLANET
JAPAN 1992
CD:Yuji Imanishi D:Patrick Glover
CL:The Planet Plan,Inc.

FRONT 　　　　　　　　　　　　　　　BACK

AN FRANCISCO OSAKA 052 NEW YORK MILAN

MIAMI LOS ANGELES HONG KONG BOSTON P

FRONT　　　　　　　　　　　　　　BACK

CAPTAIN PLANET ▲
JAPAN 1992
CD:Yuji Imanishi D:Patrick Glover
CL:The Planet Plan,Inc.

▼ **CLUB KING**
JAPAN 1991
D:See Gee Gen CL:Club King Co.

FRONT　　　　　　　　　　　　　　BACK

DALLAS AMSTERDAM PHILADELPHIA 053 LO

FRONT　　　　　　　　　　　　　　　　　　　　BACK

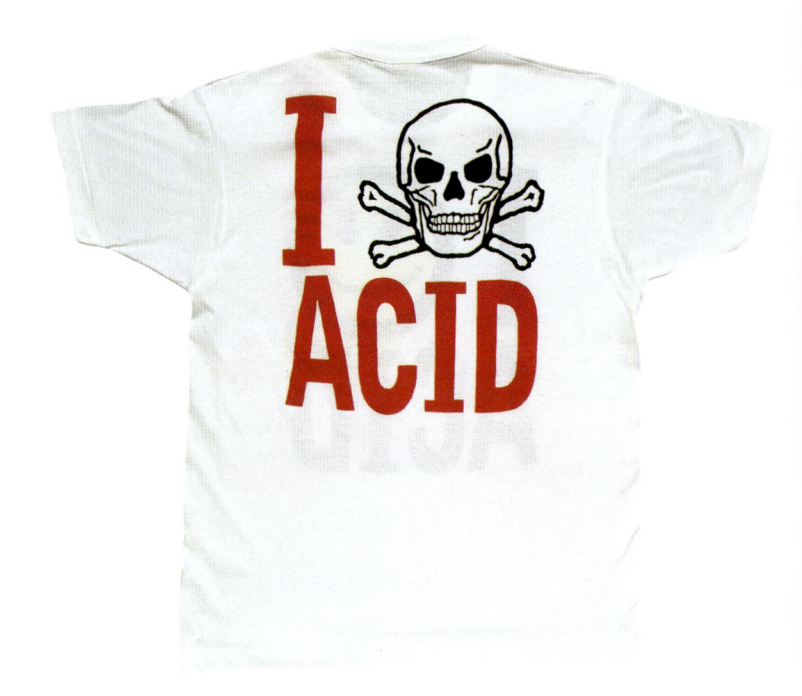

BOY ▲
UK 1988
D:Malcolm Garrett DF:Assorted Images
CL:Boy Clothing

▼ HOLLYWOOD RANCH MARKET
JAPAN 1992
CL:Seilin & Co.,

FRONT　　　　　　　　　　　　　　　　　　　　BACK

I LOS ANGELES HONG KONG BOSTON PARIS

HOLLYWOOD RANCH MARKET
JAPAN 1989-1992
CL:Seilin & Co.,

S AMSTERDAM 055 PHILADELPHIA LONDON

FLOWERS
JAPAN 1992
CL:Lemon Co.,Ltd.

FLOWERS
JAPAN 1992
CL:Lemon Co.,Ltd.

CAPTAIN PLANET
JAPAN 1992
CD,D:Yuji Imanishi CL:The Planet Plan,Inc.

GRANDPA'S PRESENT
JAPAN 1992
D,I:Tomoko Ikumi DF:Atelier Neu!! Inc.
CL:Maruzeniya Co.,Ltd.

HOLLYWOOD RANCH MARKET
JAPAN 1991
CL:Seilin & Co.,

45RPM STUDIO
JAPAN 1991
AD,D,I:Joji Yano CL:45RPM Studio Co.,Ltd.

HOW TO?
JAPAN 1992
D,I:Keiko Habara DF:Atelier Neu!! Inc.
CL:St.Evance Co.,Ltd.

45RPM STUDIO
JAPAN 1991
AD,D,I:Joji Yano CL:45RPM Studio Co.,Ltd.

KYO SEATTLE HELSINKI MIAMI LOS ANGELES

BETTY'S BLUE
JAPAN 1992
CL:Lemon Co.,Ltd.

NEW YORK MILANO DALLAS 058 AMSTERDA

FLOWERS
JAPAN 1992
CL:Lemon Co.,Ltd.

SKIP-A-BEAT
USA 1991
AD,D,I:Skip Bolen DF:Skip Bolen Studio
CL:Skip Bolen Studio

BETTY'S BLUE
JAPAN 1992
CL:Lemon Co.,Ltd.

BETTY'S BLUE
JAPAN 1992
CL:Lemon Co.,Ltd.

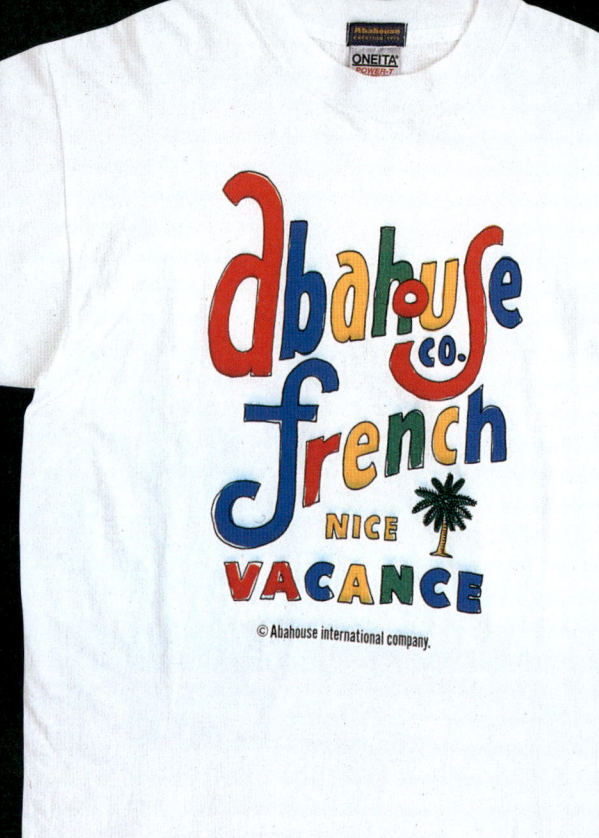

ABAHOUSE
JAPAN 1992
CD:Kiyohiro Hara D,I:Makoto Shibata
CL:Abahouse International Company

NG BOSTON PARIS SAN FRANCISCO OSAKA N

SAB STREET
JAPAN 1992
CL:Aterier Sab Co.,Ltd.

BETTY'S BLUE
JAPAN 1992
CL:Lemon Co.,Ltd.

DOUBLE FACE
USA 1991
D:Kyoko Yabuki I/R:Thirty-Three

BETTY'S BLUE
JAPAN 1992
CL:Lemon Co.,Ltd.

PHIA LONDON 061 SYDNEY ATLANTA FERRA

HELSINKI MIAMI LOS ANGELES HONG KONG BO

OZONE COMMUNITY
JAPAN 1992
CL:Ozone Community Co.,Ltd.

MARTINE SITBON FANTASY
JAPAN 1992
D:Martine Sitbon CL:The Ellebis,Ltd

BUNKAYA ZAKKATEN
THAILAND 1992
I/R:Bunkaya Zakkaten

BUNKAYA ZAKKATEN
THAILAND 1992
I/R:Bunkaya Zakkaten

LANO DALLAS AMSTERDAM 062 PHILADELPH

TON PARIS SAN FRANCISCO OSAKA NEW YOR

HYSTERIC GLAMOUR
JAPAN 1992
D:Nobuhiko Kitamura
CL:Ozone Community Co.,Ltd.

BUNKAYA ZAKKATEN
THAILAND 1992
I/R:Bunkaya Zakkaten

BUNKAYA ZAKKATEN
THAILAND 1992
I/R:Bunkaya Zakkaten

BUNKAYA ZAKKATEN
THAILAND 1992
I/R:Bunkaya Zakkaten

LONDON SYDNEY ATLANTA 063 FERRARA TO

MIAMI LOS ANGELES HONG KONG BOSTON

BUNKAYA ZAKKATEN
THAILAND 1992
I/R:Bunkaya Zakkaten

BUNKAYA ZAKKATEN
THAILAND 1992
I/R:Bunkaya Zakkaten

BUNKAYA ZAKKATEN
THAILAND 1992
I/R:Bunkaya Zakkaten

ARCHAIC SMILE
USA 1992
D:Rachel-Jeff

LAS 064 AMSTERDAM PHILADELPHIA LONDON

BUNKAYA ZAKKATEN ▲
THAILAND 1992
I/R:Bunkaya Zakkaten

▼ **BUNKAYA ZAKKATEN**
THAILAND 1992
I/R:Bunkaya Zakkaten

LOS ANGELES HONG KONG BOSTON PARIS SAN

BUNKAYA ZAKKATEN ▲
THAILAND 1992
I/R:Bunkaya Zakkaten

▼ **RED OR DEAD**
UK 1992
D:Kate Cullinan,Gary Page CL:Red or Dead

TERDAM PHILADELPHIA 066 LONDON SYDNE

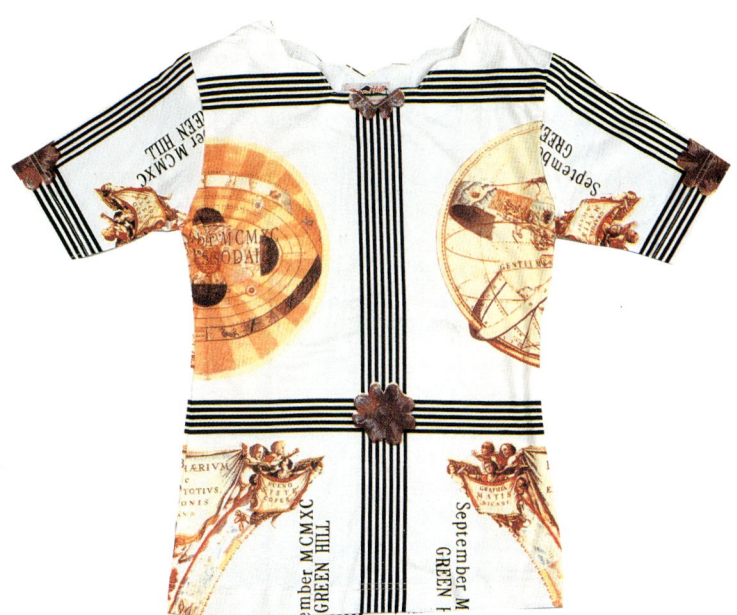

BUNKAYA ZAKKATEN
 THAILAND 1992
 I/R:Bunkaya Zakkaten

BUNKAYA ZAKKATEN
 THAILAND 1992
 I/R:Bunkaya Zakkaten

BUNKAYA ZAKKATEN
 JAPAN 1992
 CL:Bunkaya Zakkaten

BUNKAYA ZAKKATEN
 THAILAND 1992
 I/R:Bunkaya Zakkaten

HYSTERIC GLAMOUR
JAPAN 1992
D:Nobuhiko Kitamura
CL:Ozone Community Co.,Ltd.

HYSTERIC GLAMOUR
JAPAN 1992
D:Nobuhiko Kitamura
CL:Ozone Community Co.,Ltd.

HYSTERIC GLAMOUR
JAPAN 1992
D:Nobuhiko Kitamura
CL:Ozone Community Co.,Ltd.

HYSTERIC GLAMOUR
JAPAN 1992
D:Nobuhiko Kitamura
CL:Ozone Community Co.,Ltd.

SCO OSAKA NEW YORK MILANO DALLAS AMS

MILK
JAPAN 1992
CL:Milk Inc.,

MILK BOY
JAPAN 1992
CL:Milk Inc.,

MILK BOY
JAPAN 1992
CL:Milk Inc.,

MILK BOY
JAPAN 1992
CL:Milk Inc.,

NTA 069 FERRARA TOKYO SEATTLE HELSINK

POWDER
JAPAN 1992
D:Hideki Shimosako

CAN TWO
JAPAN 1992
D:Chinatsu Kishiue I:Rieko Mukai
CL:Tokyo Can Co.,Ltd.

POWDER
JAPAN 1992
D:Hideki Shimosako

GIRLFRIEND!
USA 1991
D:Nicholas Graham DF:Joe Boxer Corp.

SCOOP
JAPAN 1992
I:Konomi Tanaka,Daisuke Suzuki CL:Scoop Inc.

CAN TWO
JAPAN 1992
D:Chinatsu Kishiue I:Keiko Habara
DF:Atelier Neu!! Inc. CL:Tokyo Can Co.,Ltd.

CACHALOT
JAPAN 1991
CD:Yoko Fukawa D,I:Keiko Habara
DF:Atelier Neu!! Inc. CL:Sigma Co.,Ltd.

CACHALOT
JAPAN 1991
CD:Yoko Fukawa D,I:Keiko Habara
DF:Atelier Neu!! Inc. CL:Sigma Co.,Ltd.

POWDER
JAPAN 1992
D:Hideki Shimosako

YORK MILANO DALLAS AMSTERDAM PHILAD

POWDER
JAPAN 1992
D:Hideki Shimosako

POWDER
JAPAN 1992
D:Hideki Shimosako

POWDER
JAPAN 1992
D:Hideki Shimosako

PERSON'S
JAPAN 1992
CL:Person's Co.,Ltd.

BA-TSU CLUB
JAPAN 1992
CL:Ba-tsu Co.,Ltd.

BA-TSU CLUB
JAPAN 1992
CL:Ba-tsu Co.,Ltd.

MEN'S BA-TSU
JAPAN 1990
CL:Ba-tsu Co.,Ltd.

CAN TWO
JAPAN 1991
CD,D:Eiko Takagaki I:Keiko Habara
DF:Atelier Neu!! Inc.
CL:Tokyo Can Co.,Ltd.

MEN'S BA-TSU
JAPAN 1992
CL:Ba-tsu Co.,Ltd.

MEN'S BA-TSU
JAPAN 1990
CL:Ba-tsu Co.,Ltd.

45RPM STUDIO
JAPAN 1989
AD,D,:Joji Yano I:Hirosi Masuyama
CL:45RPM Studio Co.,Ltd.

SKIP-A-BEAT
USA 1991
AD,D,I:Skip Bolen DF:Skip Bolen Studio
CL:Skip Bolen Studio

HOLLYWOOD RANCH MARKET
JAPAN 1990
CL:Seilin & Co.,

HOLLYWOOD RANCH MARKET
JAPAN 1989
CL:Seilin & Co.,

POU DOU DOU
JAPAN 1992
D:Pou Dou Dou CL:Galerie de Pop Co.,Ltd.

POU DOU DOU
JAPAN 1992
D:Pou Dou Dou CL:Galerie de Pop Co.,Ltd.

FLOWERS
JAPAN 1992
CL:Lemon Co.,Ltd.

45RPM STUDIO
JAPAN 1991
AD,I:Joji Yano CL:45RPM Studio Co.,Ltd.

GRANDPA'S PRESENT
JAPAN 1992
D,I:Tomoko Ikumi DF:Atelier Neu!! Inc.
CL:Maruzeniya Co.,Ltd.

GRANDPA'S PRESENT
JAPAN 1992
D,I:Tomoko Ikumi DF:Atelier Neu!! Inc.
CL:Maruzeniya Co.,Ltd.

COCONUTS ISLAND
JAPAN
CD:Akio Hidejima AD:Lion & D:Chikako Ushikai
I:Yuichi Bando,Miyoko Sato,Akio Hidejima PR:J Club
DF:Coconuts Company

STERDAM PHILADELPHIA LONDON SYDNEY AT

MEN'S BIGI
JAPAN 1992
CL:Men's Bigi Co.,Ltd.

HOW TO?
JAPAN 1992
AD,D,I:Michiaki Akiyama DF:St.Evance Co.,Ltd.

THE GINZA/ITO SACHICO
JAPAN 1992
D,I:Sachico Ito DF:Sugar Inc CL:The Ginza

MEN'S MELROSE
JAPAN 1992
I:Timney-Fowler Limited CL:Melrose Co.,Ltd.

LOS ANGELES HONG KONG BOSTON 079 PAR

SAKA NEW YORK MILANO DALLAS AMSTERDA

JOE BOXER CORP.
USA 1991
D:Nicholas Graham

GIRLFRIEND!
USA 1992
D:Nicholas Graham DF:Joe Boxer Corp.

BUNKAYA ZAKKATEN
JAPAN 1992
CL:Bunkaya Zakkaten

BUNKAYA ZAKKATEN
JAPAN 1992
CL:Bunkaya Zakkaten

A TOKYO 080 SEATTLE HELSINKI MIAMI LOS

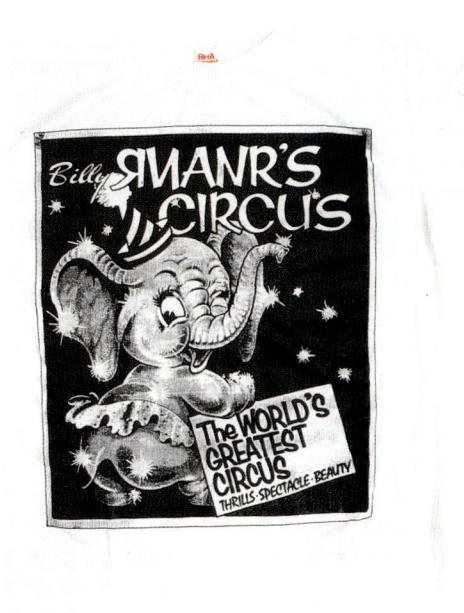

CANE HAUL ROAD
USA 1989
D,I:Grant Kagimoto CL:Cane Haul Road,Ltd.

RNA
JAPAN 1992
CL:RNA Inc.

KEN BROWN
USA 1991
D:Ken Brown DF:Ken Brown Designs

BUNKAYA ZAKKATEN
JAPAN 1992
CL:Bunkaya Zakkaten

FELIX THE CAT
JAPAN 1992
AD,D,I:Keiko Habara DF:Atelier Neu!! Inc.
CL:St.Evance Co.,Ltd.

THUNDERBIRDS
JAPAN 1992
CL:Cizna Inc.

HERCULOIDS
JAPAN 1992
CL:Cizna Inc.

DUCKMAN
USA 1990
D,I:Everett Peck DF:Richard W.Salzman Artist Representative
CL:Therapy Springs Presents

BODY RAP
UK 1992
D:Me Company

BODY RAP
UK 1992
D:Me Company

BUNKAYA ZAKKATEN
JAPAN 1992
CL:Bunkaya Zakkaten

SCOOP
JAPAN 1992
I:Studio 9 Inch, Kyuhei Murayama
CL:Scoop Inc.

SWIFTY
UK 1991
AD,D:Ian Swift DF:Swifty Typographics
CL:Swifty Favourite Gears

PAUL SMITH
JAPAN 1992
D:Paul Smith CL:Joi'x Corporation

PERSON'S
JAPAN 1992
CL:Person's Co.,Ltd.

FLOWERS
JAPAN 1992
CL:Lemon Co.,Ltd.

F·B·I & S·P.CO.
JAPAN 1992
CD:Takahisa Kamiya AD:Etsuro Kusunoki
D:Isao Okochi CL:Super Planning Co.,Ltd.

BA-TSU
JAPAN 1992
CL:Ba-tsu Co.,Ltd.

CONSCIONS MESSAGES
USA 1990
CD,D:Gail Rigelhaupt CD:Harris Silver
DF:Rigelhaupt Design

CLUB KING
JAPAN 1989
D:Club King CL:Club King Co.

TRADERS
JAPAN 1992
CD,D:Yasushi Inoue I:Keiko Habara
DF:Atelier Neu!! Inc. CL:Nakane Yasu Co.,Ltd.

CLUB KING
JAPAN 1991
I:Hirosuke Ueno
CL:Club King Co.

SKIP-A-BEAT
USA 1991
AD,D,I:Skip Bolen DF:Skip Bolen Studio
CL:Skip Bolen Studio

SKIP-A-BEAT
USA 1990
AD,D,I:Skip Bolen DF:Skip Bolen Studio
CL:Skip Bolen Studio

CLUB KING
JAPAN 1991
I:Hirosuke Ueno
CL:Club King Co.

STERDAM PHILADELPHIA LONDON SYDNEY A

FRONT

BACK

KANSAI O2
JAPAN 1992
D:Kansai Company CL:Kansai Company

KANSAI O2
JAPAN 1992
D:Kansai Company CL:Kansai Company

KANSAI O2
JAPAN 1992
D:Kansai Company CL:Kansai Company

S ANGELES HONG KONG BOSTON 088 PARIS

KANSAI O2
JAPAN 1992
D:Kansai Company CL:Kansai Company

KANSAI O2
JAPAN 1992
D:Kansai Company CL:Kansai Company

TYCOON
JAPAN 1991
D:Toshio Nakanishi CL:Club King Co.

RNA
JAPAN 1992
CL:RNA Inc.

ATELIER SAB FOR MEN
JAPAN 1992
D:Akio Kurokawa CL:Aterier Sab Co.,Ltd.

5351 POUR LES HOMMES
JAPAN 1992
CD:Kiyohiro Hara AD,D:Makoto Shibata
CL:Abahouse International Company

ATELIER SAB FOR MEN
JAPAN 1992
D:Akio Kurokawa CL:Aterier Sab Co.,Ltd.

5351 POUR LES HOMMES
JAPAN 1992
CD:Kiyohiro Hara AD,D:Makoto Shibata
CL:Abahouse International Company

ERRARA TOKYO SEATTLE HELSINKI MIAMI LO

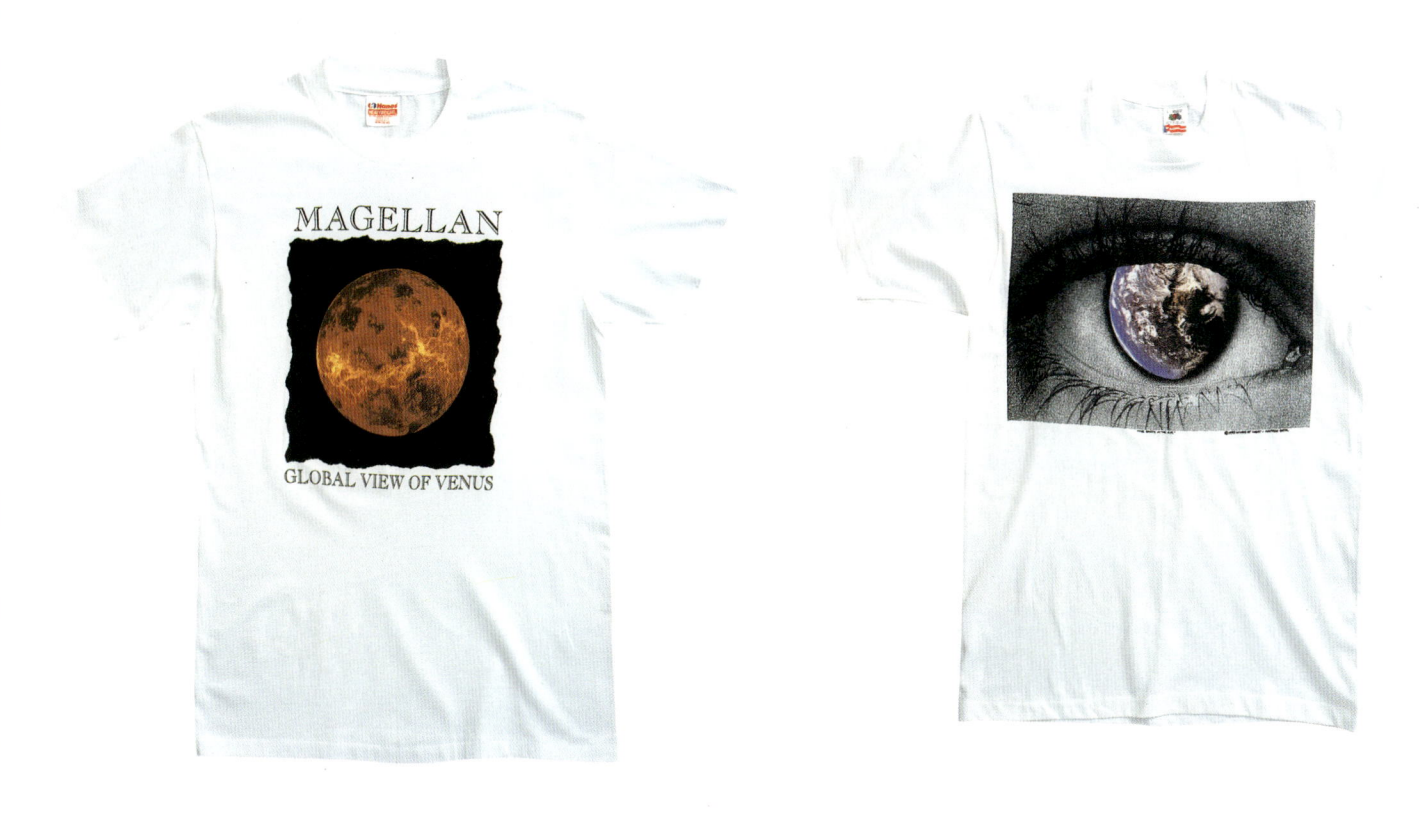

JET PROPULSION LABORATORY
USA 1992
D:Coastal Printworks,Inc. P:Coastal Printworks,Inc.

POU DOU DOU
JAPAN 1992
D:Pou Dou Dou CL:Galerie de Pop Co.,Ltd.

EYE
USA 1991
D:Los Angeles T-Shirt Museum

5351 POUR LES HOMMES
JAPAN 1992
CD:Kiyohiro Hara AD,D:Makoto Shibata
CL:Abahouse International Company

SAKA NEW YORK MILANO 091 DALLAS AMST

LONDON SYDNEY ATLANTA FERRARA TOKYO S

F·B·I & S·P.CO.
JAPAN 1992
CD:Takahisa Kamiya AD:Etsuro Kusunoki
D:Isao Okochi CL:Super Planning Co.,Ltd.

CAPTAIN PLANET
JAPAN 1992
CD,D:Yuji Imanishi
CL:The Planet Plan,Inc.

45RPM STUDIO
JAPAN 1991
AD,D,I:Joji Yano CL:45RPM Studio Co.,Ltd.

OCTOPUS ARMY
JAPAN 1991
D:Hiroto Kitamura P:Kazuyoshi Miyoshi

OSTON PARIS 092 SAN FRANCISCO OSAKA N

MEN'S MELROSE
JAPAN 1992
CL:Melrose Co.,Ltd.

PERSON'S FOR MEN
JAPAN 1992
CL:Person's Co.,Ltd.

PERSON'S
JAPAN 1992
CL:Person's Co.,Ltd.

MEN'S MELROSE
JAPAN 1992
CL:Melrose Co.,Ltd.

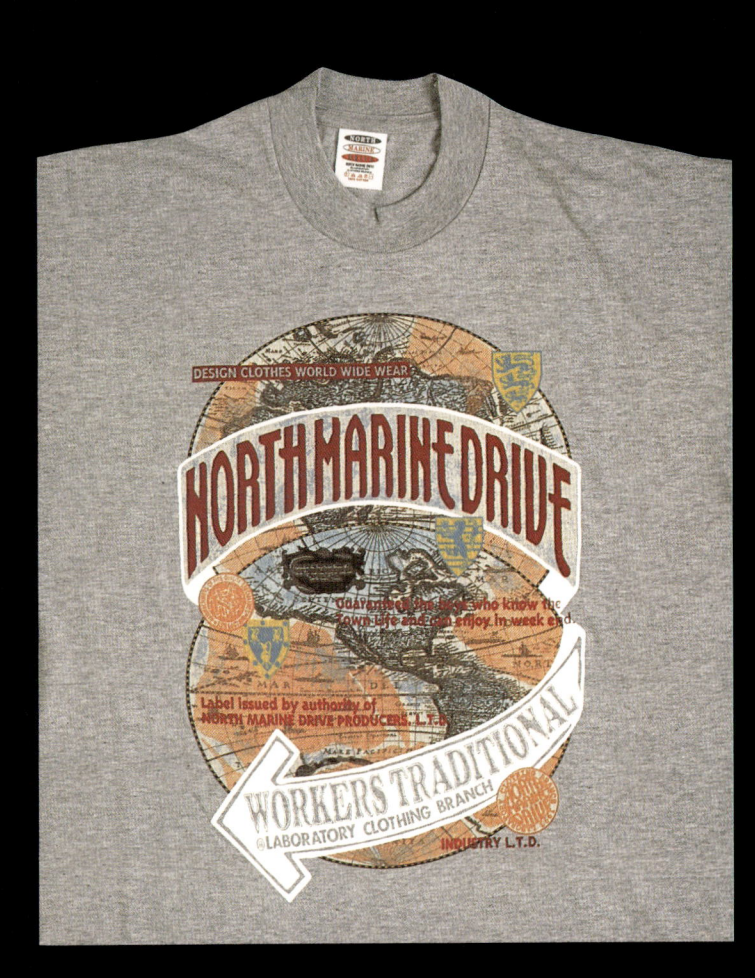

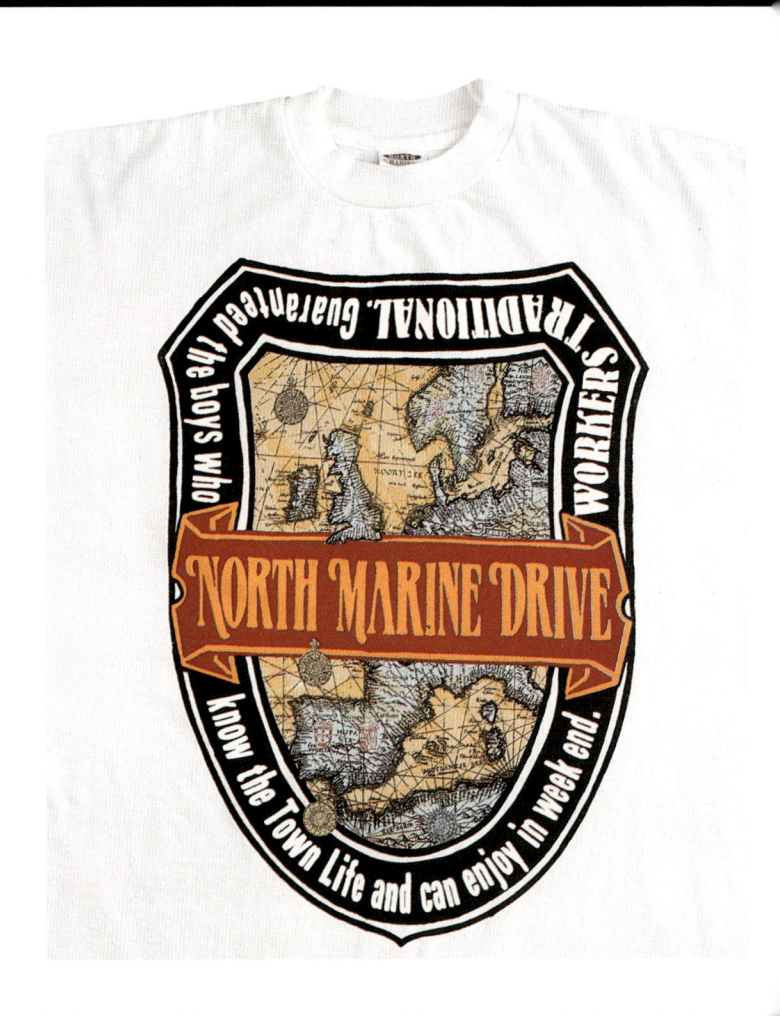

NORTH MARINE DRIVE
JAPAN 1991
AD,D,I:Joji Yano CL:45RPM Studio Co.,Ltd.

PERSON'S
JAPAN 1992
CL:Person's Co.,Ltd.

PERSON'S
JAPAN 1992
CL:Person's Co.,Ltd.

NORTH MARINE DRIVE
JAPAN 1991
AD,D:Joji Yano CL:45RPM Studio Co.,Ltd.

HOLLYWOOD RANCH MARKET
JAPAN 1985
CL:Seilin & Co.,

NATURE COMPANY
USA 1987
AD,D:Kit Hinrichs DF:Pentagram Design

SPEEDO
USA 1988
AD,D:Kit Hinrichs DF:Pentagram Design

NATURE COMPANY
USA 1987
AD,D:Kit Hinrichs DF:Pentagram Design

SPEEDO
USA 1988
AD,D:Kit Hinrichs DF:Pentagram Design

I MIAMI LOS ANGELES HONG KONG BOSTON

FRONT BACK

MEN'S BA-TSU
JAPAN 1992
CL:Ba-tsu Co.,Ltd.

SISLEY
ITALY 1992
CL:Benetton SpA

SKIP-A-BEAT
USA 1992
AD,D,I:Skip Bolen DF:Skip Bolen Studio
CL:Skip Bolen Studio

DALLAS AMSTERDAM PHILADELPHIA 097 LON

ROCKIN T
UK 1992
D:Tony Jennings of Newart

ROCKIN T
UK 1992
D:Tony Jennings of Newart

ROCKIN T
UK 1992
D:Tony Jennings of Newart

ROCKIN T
UK 1992
D:Tony Jennings of Newart

LOS ANGELES HONG KONG BOSTON PARIS S

ROCKIN T
UK 1992
D:Tony Jennings of Newart

ROCKIN T
UK 1992
D:Tony Jennings of Newart

ROCKIN T
UK 1992
D:Tony Jennings of Newart

ROCKIN T
UK 1992
D:Tony Jennings of Newart

AMSTERDAM 099 PHILADELPHIA LONDON S

ARA TOKYO SEATTLE HELSINKI MIAMI LOS A

ROCKIN T
UK 1992
D:Tony Jennings of Newart

THUNDERBIRDS
JAPAN 1992
CL:Cizna Inc.

HANK PLAYER
USA 1992
D:Sander Weintraub I:Scott Ogden
P:Coastal Printworks,Inc.

HANK PLAYER
USA 1992
D:Sander Weintraub I:Scott Ogden
P:Coastal Printworks,Inc.

O OSAKA NEW YORK 100 MILANO DALLAS AM

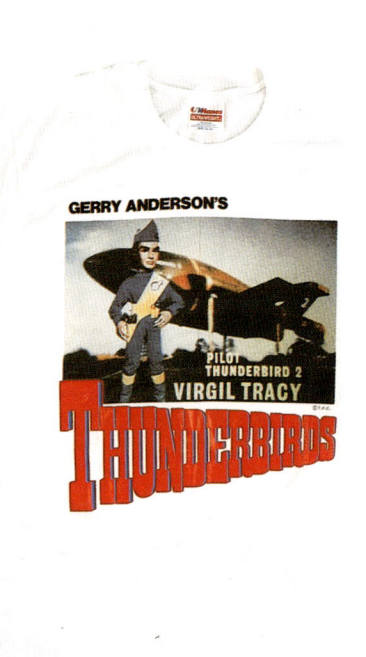

HANK PLAYER
USA 1991
D:Sander Weintraub I:Scott Ogden
P:Coastal Printworks,Inc.

HANK PLAYER
USA 1991
D:Sander Weintraub I:Scott Ogden
P:Coastal Printworks,Inc.

HANK PLAYER
USA 1991
D:Sander Weintraub I:Scott Ogden
P:Coastal Printworks,Inc.

HANK PLAYER
USA 1991
D:Sander Weintraub I:Scott Ogden
P:Coastal Printworks,Inc.

YO SEATTLE HELSINKI MIAMI LOS ANGELES

ESPRIT
USA 1989
CD,D,I:Jennifer Morla
DF:Morla Design,Inc. CL:Esprit de Corp

NEW YORK MILANO DALLAS 102 AMSTERDA

ICE ▲
PORTUGAL 1991
AD,D:Antero Ferreira
DF:Antero Ferreira Design CL:Infesveste

▼ **RENO DESIGN GROUP**
AUSTRALIA 1992
AD,D,I:Graham Rendoth DF:Reno Design Group

TTLE HELSINKI MIAMI LOS ANGELES HONG K

SISLEY
ITALY 1992
CL:Benetton SpA

K 104 MILANO DALLAS AMSTERDAM PHILAD

MINI BA-TSU
JAPAN 1988 - 1991
CL:Ba-tsu Co.,Ltd

BENETTON
ITALY 1992
CL:Benetton SpA

BENETTON
ITALY 1992
CL:Benetton SpA

BENETTON
ITALY 1992
CL:Benetton SpA

FRONT

BACK

TON PARIS SAN FRANCISCO OSAKA NEW YO

FRONT　　　　　　　　　　　　　　　　　BACK

▲ BENETTON
ITALY 1992
CL: Benetton SpA

▼ BENETTON
ITALY 1992
CL: Benetton SpA

BACK

FRONT

LONDON SYDNEY ATLANTA 107 FERRARA TO

MIAMI LOS ANGELES HONG KONG BOSTON

NIKE
USA
D,I:Angela Snow CL:Nike,Inc.

NIKE
USA 1992
I/R:World Sports Plaza

NIKE
USA 1992
I/R:World Sports Plaza

NIKE
USA 1992
I/R:World Sports Plaza

LAS 108 AMSTERDAM PHILADELPHIA LONDO

GOLDRUSH BASKETBALL
USA 1991
D:Los Angeles T-Shirt Museum

SALEM
USA 1992
I/R:World Sports Plaza

SALEM
USA 1992
I/R:World Sports Plaza

FRONT

BACK

MICHAEL JORDAN-CHICAGO
USA 1991
D:Los Angeles T-Shirt Museum

SALEM
USA 1992
I/R:World Sports Plaza

NIKE
USA
D,I:Angela Snow CL:Nike,Inc.

NIKE
USA
D,I:Angela Snow CL:Nike,Inc.

FRANCISCO OSAKA NEW YORK MILANO DALLA

FRONT　　　　　　　　　　　　　　　　BACK

NIKE ▲
USA
D,I:Angela Snow CL:Nike,Inc.

▼ **NIKE**
USA
D,I:Angela Snow CL:Nike,Inc.

FRONT 　　　　　　　　　　　　　　　　BACK

ATLANTA FERRARA 111 TOKYO SEATTLE HEL

SALEM
USA 1992
I/R:World Sports Plaza

SALEM
USA 1992
I/R:World Sports Plaza

SALEM
USA 1992
I/R:East Point Co.,Ltd.

SALEM
USA 1992
I/R:World Sports Plaza

CO OSAKA NEW YORK MILANO DALLAS AMST

GAPSTAR
NETHERLANDS 1991
D:Boy Bastiaens CL:Bigstar International

LOGO 7
USA 1992
I/R:World Sports Plaza

LOGO 7
USA 1992
I/R:World Sports Plaza

LOGO 7
USA 1992
I/R:World Sports Plaza

FERRARA TOKYO SEATTLE HELSINKI

FRONT　　　　　　　　　　　　　　　　　　BACK

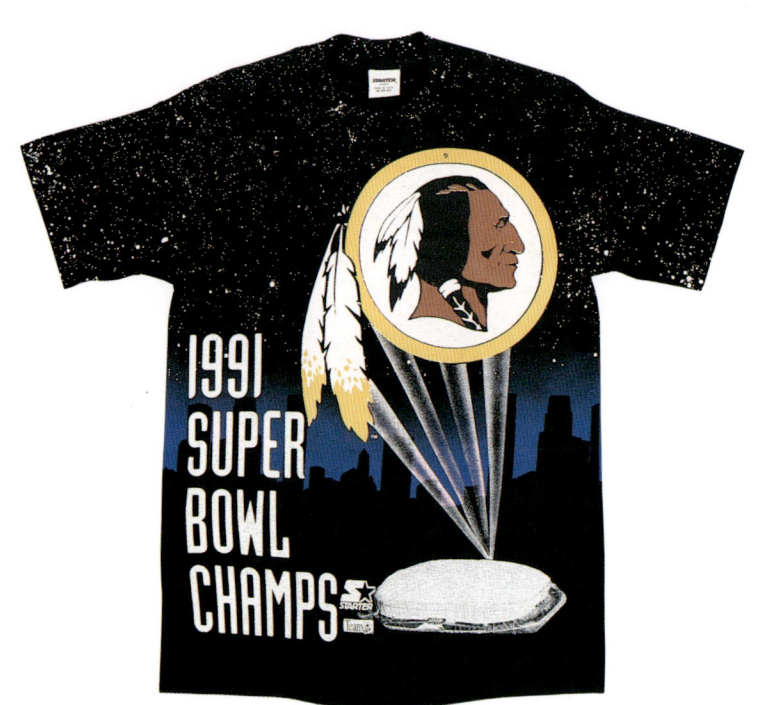

STARTER ▲
USA 1992
I/R:World Sports Plaza

▼ SALEM
USA 1992
I/R:World Sports Plaza

FRONT 　　　　　　　　　　　　　　　　　　BACK

NEW YORK MILANO DALLAS AMSTERDAM P

FRONT BACK

XPLOSION ▲
USA
I/R: World Sports Plaza

▼ SALEM
USA 1992
I/R: East Point Co., Ltd.

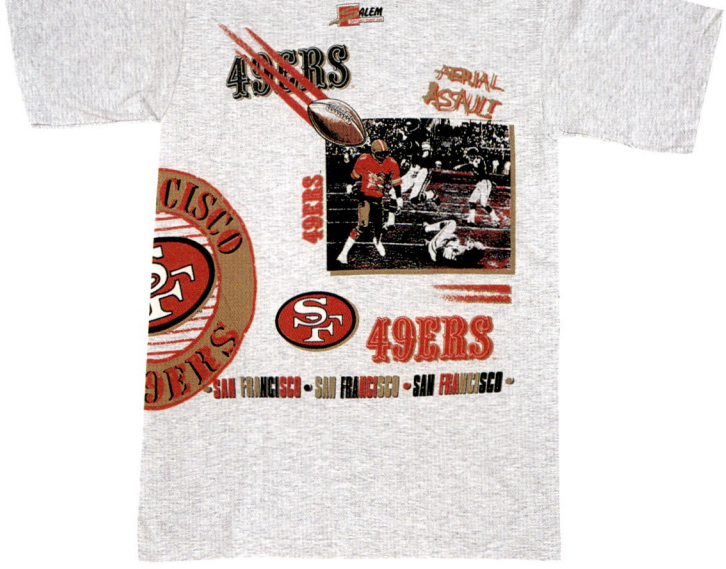

FRONT BACK

TOKYO 115 SEATTLE HELSINKI MIAMI LOS

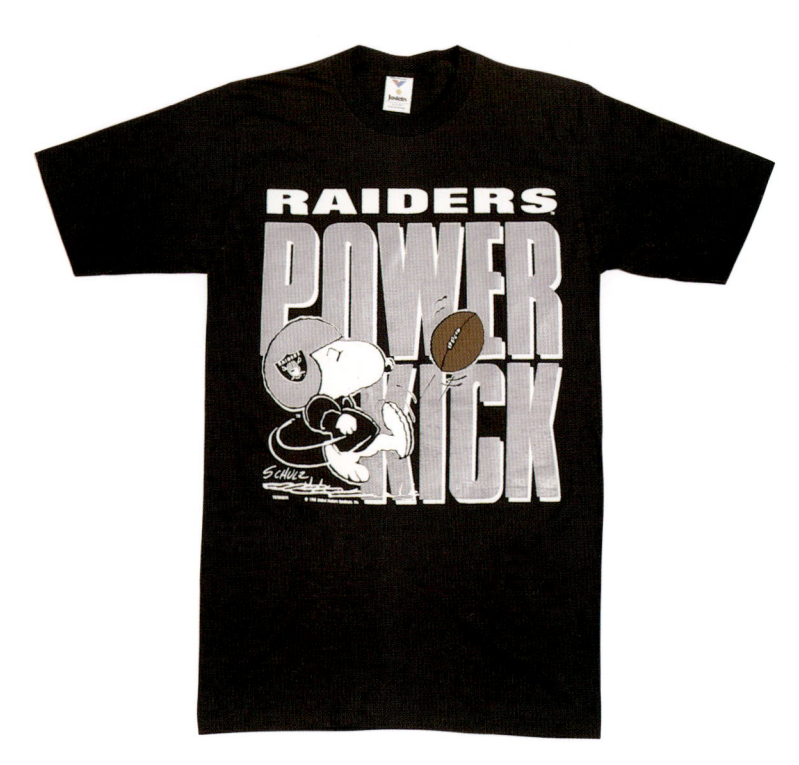

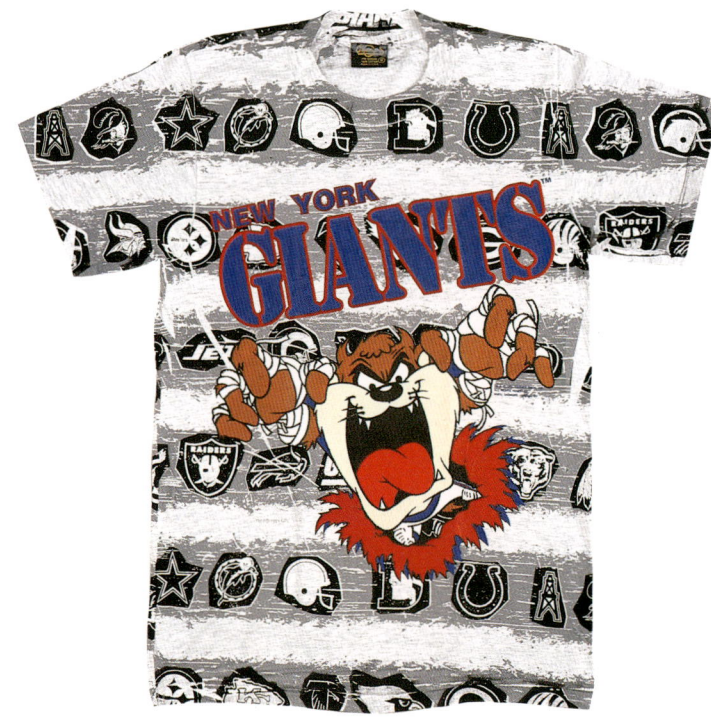

JOSTENS
USA 1992
I/R:World Sports Plaza

CHANGES
USA 1992
I/R:World Sports Plaza

CHANGES
USA 1992
I/R:World Sports Plaza

W.S.P.ORIGINAL
JAPAN 1992
CL:World Sports Plaza

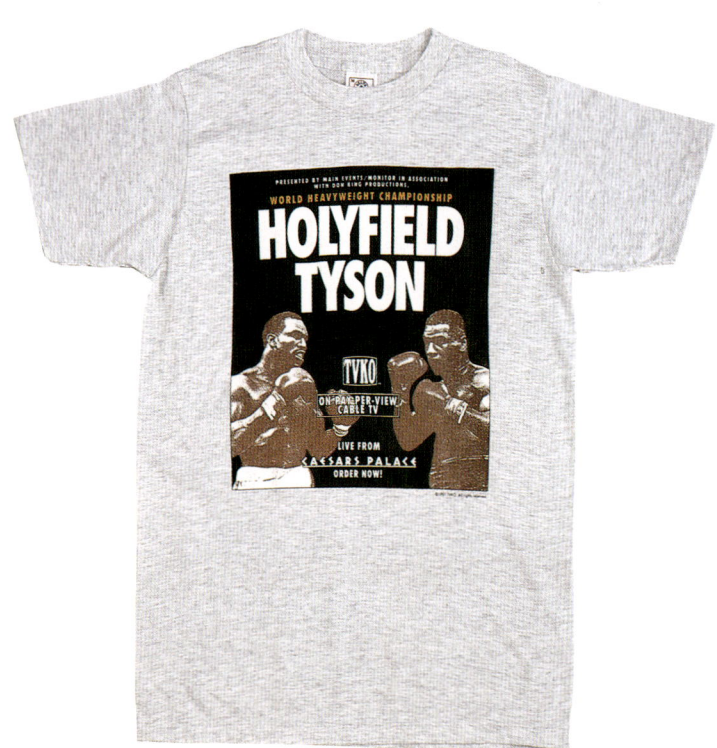

YORK MILANO DALLAS AMSTERDAM PHILAD

HUNNER SPORTSWEAR
USA 1992
I/R:World Sports Plaza

KINETIC DESIGN
USA 1992
I/R:East Point Co.,Ltd.

MAGIC JOHNSON
USA 1992
I/R:World Sports Plaza

KINETIC DESIGN
USA 1992
I/R:East Point Co.,Ltd.

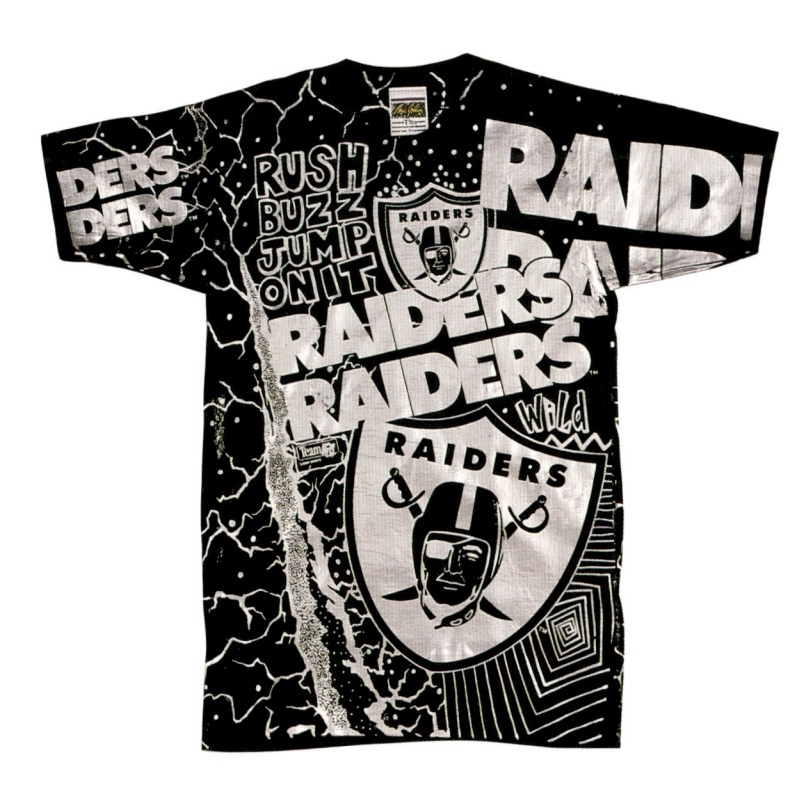

KYO SEATTLE HELSINKI MIAMI 117 LOS ANGE

N PARIS SAN FRANCISCO OSAKA NEW YORK

FRONT　　　　　　　　　　　　　　BACK

STARTER
USA 1992
I/R:World Sports Plaza

MAJESTIC
USA 1992
I/R:World Sports Plaza

SALEM
USA 1992
I/R:World Sports Plaza

118 SYDNEY ATLANTA FERRARA TOKYO S

LANO DALLAS AMSTERDAM PHILADELPHIA L

SALEM
USA 1992
I/R:World Sports Plaza

SALEM
USA 1992
I/R:World Sports Plaza

SALEM
USA 1992
I/R:World Sports Plaza

SALEM
USA 1992
I/R:World Sports Plaza

TTLE HELSINKI 119 MIAMI LOS ANGELES HO

STARTER
USA 1992
I/R:World Sports Plaza

LOGO 7
USA 1992
I/R:World Sports Plaza

JOSTENS
USA 1992
I/R:World Sports Plaza

SALEM
USA 1992
I/R:World Sports Plaza

DALLAS AMSTERDAM PHILADELPHIA LONDON

SALEM
USA 1992
I/R:World Sports Plaza

EAST POINT
JAPAN 1992
CL:East Point Co.,Ltd.

RUSSEL
USA 1992
I/R:East Point Co.,Ltd.

LOGO 7
USA 1992
I/R:East Point Co.,Ltd.

ELSINKI MIAMI LOS ANGELES 121 HONG KONG

NCISCO OSAKA NEW YORK MILANO DALLAS

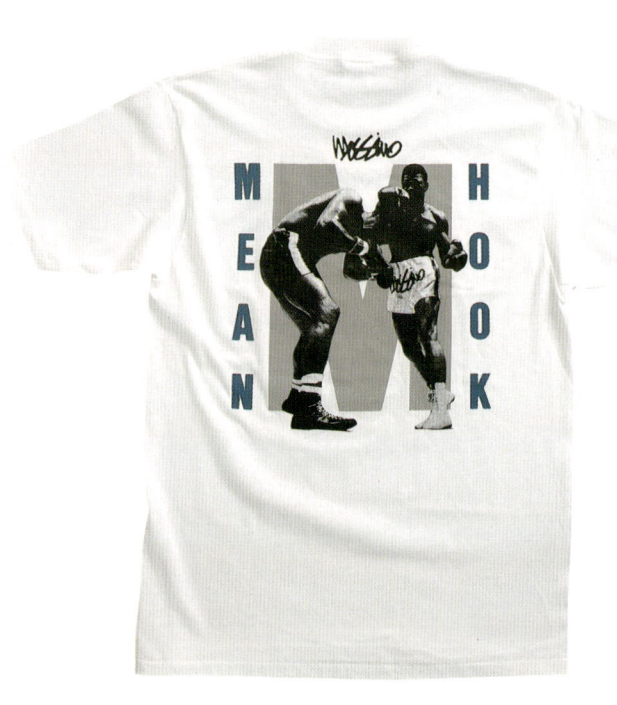

MOSSIMO
USA 1992
D:Mossimo Giannulli I:Fred Hild CL:Mossimo,Inc.

MOSSIMO
USA 1992
D:Mossimo Giannulli I:Fred Hild CL:Mossimo,Inc.

MOSSIMO
USA 1992
D:Mossimo Giannulli I:Fred Hild CL:Mossimo,Inc.

MOSSIMO
USA 1992
D:Mossimo Giannulli I:Fred Hild CL:Mossimo,Inc.

ERRARA TOKYO SEATTLE HELSINKI 122 MIA

STERDAM PHILADELPHIA LONDON SYDNEY

FRONT									BACK

NIKE
USA 1992
I/R:World Sports Plaza

STUSSY INCORPORATED
USA 1991
D,I:Shawn Stussy

STUSSY INCORPORATED
USA 1991
D,I:Shawn Stussy

LOS ANGELES HONG KONG BOSTON 123 PAR

SAKA NEW YORK MILANO DALLAS AMSTERDA

HANK PLAYER
USA 1991
D:Sander Weintraub I:Scott Ogden
P:Coastal Printworks,Inc.

HANK PLAYER
USA 1991
D:Sander Weintraub I:Scott Ogden
P:Coastal Printworks,Inc.

HANK PLAYER
USA 1992
D:Sander Weintraub I:Scott Ogden
P:Coastal Printworks,Inc.

HANK PLAYER
USA 1991
D:Sander Weintraub I:Scott Ogden
P:Coastal Printworks,Inc.

TOKYO 124 SEATTLE HELSINKI MIAMI LOS

PHILADELPHIA LONDON SYDNEY ATLANTA F

REEBOK INTERNATIONAL
USA 1991
D:Howard Idelson DF:Urban Image

GELES 125 HONG KONG BOSTON PARIS SAN

CRAZY SHIRTS
USA
D,I:Jeff Diamond CL:Crazy Shirts,Inc.

SIMPLETON
USA 1991
AD,D:Marcos Chavez
DF:Michael Stanard,Inc. CL:Millenium

GOTCHA
USA
D:Jody Radzik CL:Gotcha Sportswear

SKATE ACTION SPORTS
USA 1992
D:Rob Donnelly,Karl Maruyama DF:Rob Art,Inc.

GOTCHA
USA
D:Jody Radzik CL:Gotcha Sportswear

STORMERS
USA 1990
D,I:Ruth Wyatt,Kevin Wyatt DF:Bark Like a Dog Design

SPUTNIKS
USA 1991
D,I:Mike Owens,Kevin Wyatt DF:Delor Design Group

PSL(PACIFIC SURFLINES)
USA 1991
D:Pacific Eyes & T's CL:Pacific Eyes & T's

REN MAN (RENAISSANCE MAN)
USA 1989
AD,D:Marcos Chavez D:Mark Naden
DF:Michael Stanard,Inc. CL:Millenium

OOGA BOOGA
USA 1989
AD,D:Marcos Chavez D:Mark Naden
DF:Michael Stanard,Inc. CL:Millenium

SOME PEOPLE CAN'T SURF
USA 1989
AD,D,I:Art Chantry CL:Post-Industrial Stress+Design

CRAZY SHIRTS
USA 1989
AD,D,I:Rex Morache DF:Designosaurus Rex

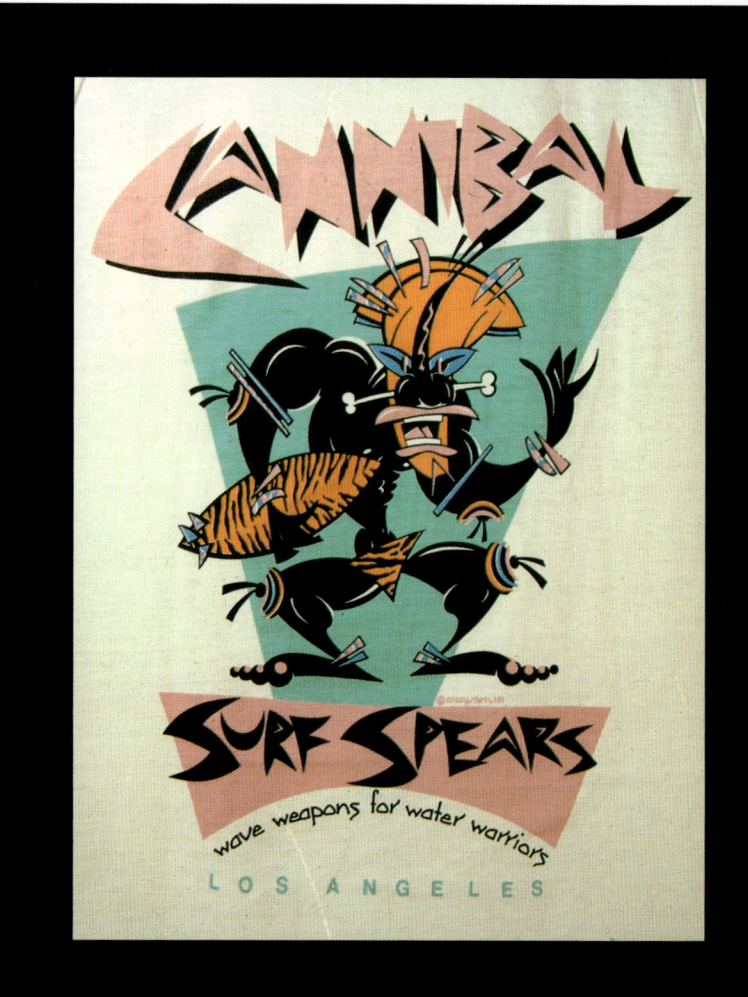

SURF MOTEL
USA 1989
AD,D,I:Art Chantry CL:Post-Industrial Stress+Design

HAPPY DEAD GUY
USA 1989
AD,D,I:Art Chantry CL:Post-Industrial Stress+Design

ZONK
USA 1990
D,I:Tracy Sabin DF:Sabin Design CL:Zonk,Inc.

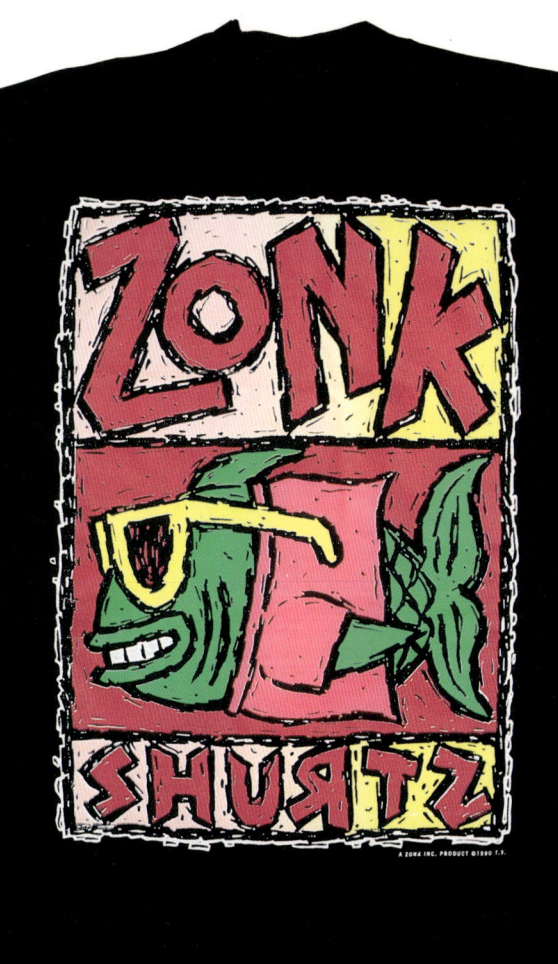

CRAZY SHIRTS
USA
D,I:Dennis Debasco CL:Crazy Shirts,Inc.

CRAZY SHIRTS
USA
D,I:Lee Samson CL:Crazy Shirts,Inc.

CALIFORNIA BEACH CO.
USA 1989
CD:Richard Sawyer D,I:Tracy Sabin DF:Sabin Design

CALIFORNIA BEACH CO.
USA 1989
CD:Richard Sawyer
D,I:Tracy Sabin DF:Sabin Design

CALIFORNIA BLUES
USA 1990
CD:John Goldsmith,Bobby Grillo
D,I:Tracy Sabin DF:Sabin Design

ZONK
USA 1990
CD:Greg Sabin D,I:Tracy Sabin
DF:Sabin Design CL:Zonk,Inc.

CALIFORNIA BLUES
USA 1990
CD:John Goldsmith,Bobby Grillo
D,I:Tracy Sabin DF:Sabin Design

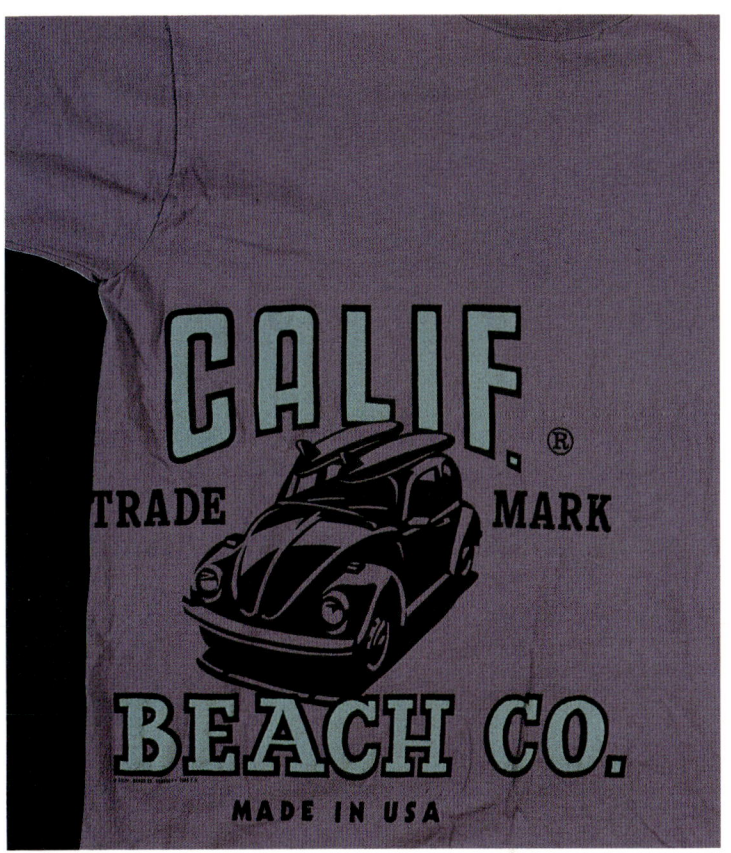

CALIFORNIA BLUES
USA 1989
CD:John Goldsmith, Bobby Grillo
D,I:Tracy Sabin DF:Sabin Design

CALIFORNIA BEACH CO.
USA 1989
CD:Richard Sawyer D,I:Tracy Sabin DF:Sabin Design

ZONK
USA 1990
CD:Greg Sabin D,I:Tracy Sabin
DF:Sabin Design CL:Zonk,Inc.

CALIFORNIA BEACH CO.
USA 1989
CD:Richard Sawyer D,I:Tracy Sabin DF:Sabin Design

PERFECT CONDITIONS
USA 1989
CD:John Goldsmith,Bobby Grillo
D,I:Tracy Sabin DF:Sabin Design CL:California Blues

CALIFORNIA BEACH CO.
USA 1989
CD:Richard Sawyer D,I:Tracy Sabin DF:Sabin Design

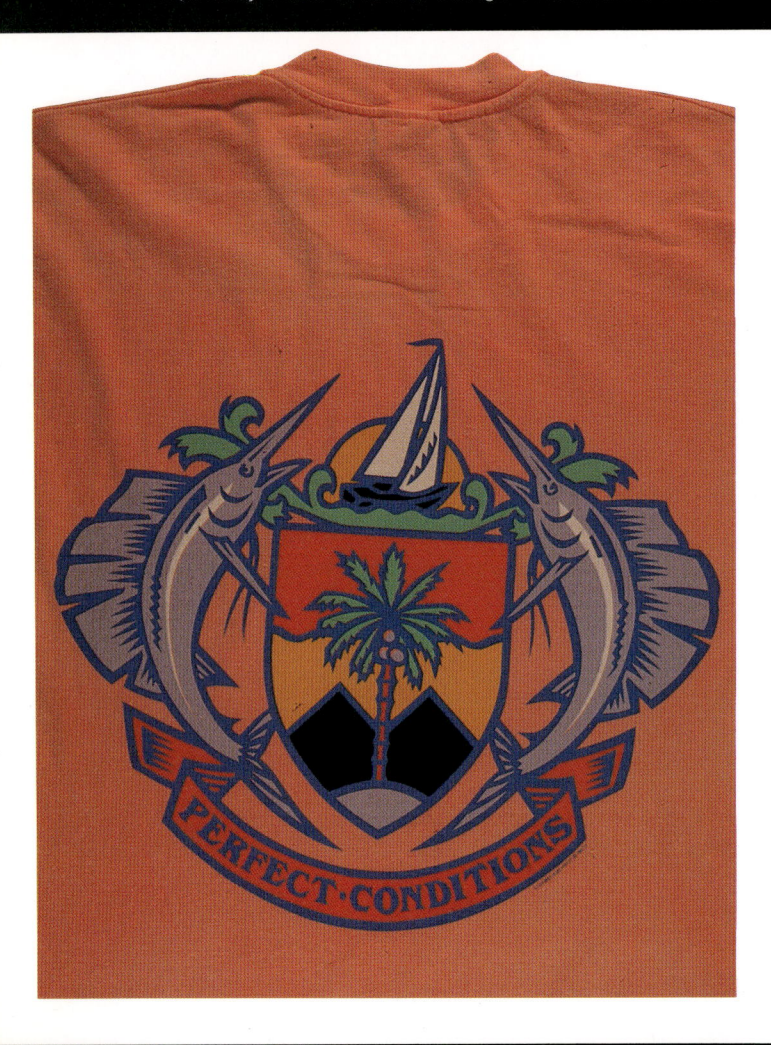

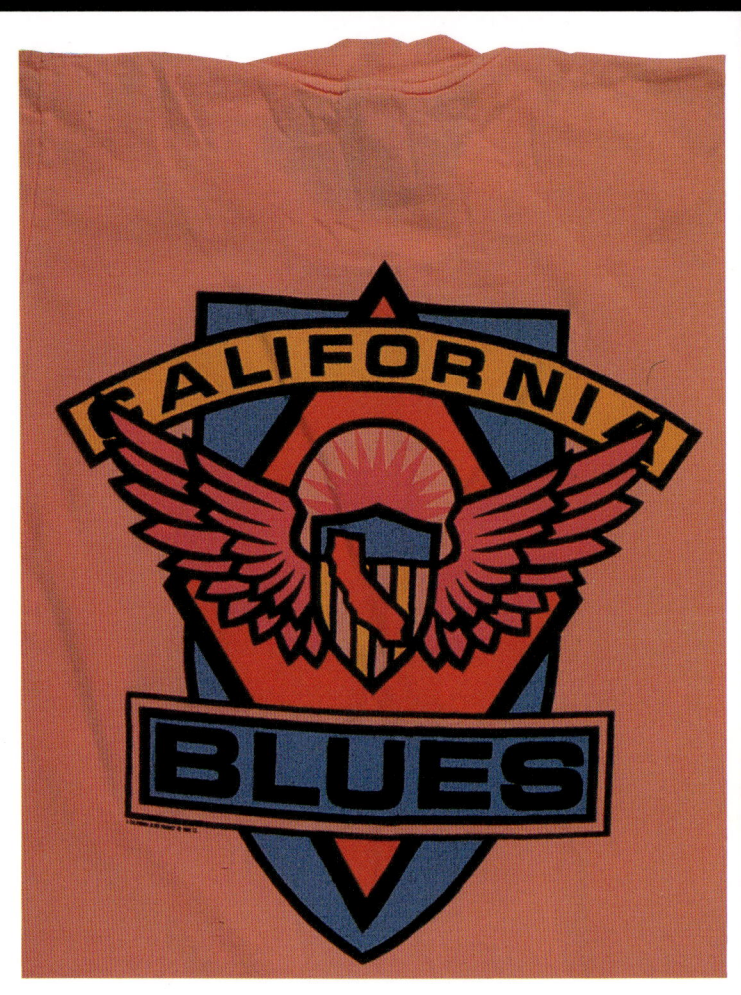

ZONK
USA 1989
CD:Greg Sabin D,I:Tracy Sabin
DF:Sabin Design CL:Zonk,Inc.

CALIFORNIA BLUES
USA 1989
CD:John Goldsmith,Bobby Grillo
D,I:Tracy Sabin DF:Sabin Design

PACIFIC POWER
AUSTRALIA 1991
AD,D,I:Emery Vincent Associates DF:Emery Vincent Associates
CL:Pacific Power New South Wales Electricity

AUSSIE
USA 1991
D:Aussie Racing Apparel
DF:Aussie Racing Apparel CL:Cycle World

AUSSIE
USA 1991
D:Aussie Racing Apparel DF:Aussie Racing Apparel

AUSSIE
USA 1992
D:Aussie Racing Apparel
DF:Aussie Racing Apparel CL:Off Road

AUSSIE
USA 1992
D:Aussie Racing Apparel
DF:Aussie Racing Apparel CL:UCLA

AUSSIE
USA 1992
D:Aussie Racing Apparel
DF:Aussie Racing Apparel CL:Velo Playa Larga

N SYDNEY ATLANTA FERRARA TOKYO SEATTL

AUSSIE
USA 1992
D:Aussie Racing Apparel
DF:Aussie Racing Apparel CL:Zen Warriors C.C.

AUSSIE
USA 1992
D:Aussie Racing Apparel
DF:Aussie Racing Apparel CL:Bike Beat

AUSSIE
USA 1991
D:Aussie Racing Apparel DF:Aussie Racing Apparel
CL:U. of Oregon

AUSSIE
USA 1991
D:Aussie Racing Apparel
DF:Aussie Racing Apparel CL:Warner Velo

N PARIS SAN FRANCISCO 138 OSAKA NEW YO

AUSSIE
USA
D:Aussie Racing Apparel
DF:Aussie Racing Apparel CL:Phoenix Consumers C.C.

AUSSIE
USA 1992
D:Aussie Racing Apparel
DF:Aussie Racing Apparel CL:Bally's

AUSSIE
USA 1992
D:Aussie Racing Apparel
DF:Aussie Racing Apparel CL:Hotter'n Hell Hundred

AUSSIE
USA 1991
D:Aussie Racing Apparel
DF:Aussie Racing Apparel CL:Mountain Goat

ATLANTA FERRARA TOKYO SEATTLE HELSIN

AUSSIE
USA 1992
D:Aussie Racing Apparel
DF:Aussie Racing Apparel CL:Hewlett Packard

AUSSIE
USA 1992
D:Aussie Racing Apparel
DF:Aussie Racing Apparel CL:Bat Wing C.C.

AUSSIE
USA 1992
D:Aussie Racing Apparel
DF:Aussie Racing Apparel CL:Red Rose C.C.

AUSSIE
USA 1991
D:Aussie Racing Apparel
DF:Aussie Racing Apparel CL:Peloton Racing

AN FRANCISCO OSAKA 140 NEW YORK MILAN

MIAMI LOS ANGELES HONG KONG BOSTON P

AUSSIE
USA
D:Aussie Racing Apparel
DF:Aussie Racing Apparel CL:Clarksville Schwinn

AUSSIE
USA 1991
D:Aussie Racing Apparel
DF:Aussie Racing Apparel CL:Specialized(CCCP)

AUSSIE
USA 1989
D:Aussie Racing Apparel
DF:Aussie Racing Apparel CL:Esprit Velo

AUSSIE
USA 1992
D:Aussie Racing Apparel
DF:Aussie Racing Apparel CL:Excel

DALLAS AMSTERDAM PHILADELPHIA 141 LON

URBAN ICONS, LONDON
USA 1990
AD,D,I:Joel Katz DF:Katz Wheeler Design
CL:Katz Wheeler Design

THE DESIGN COMPANY
USA 1988
AD,D,I:Marcia Romanuck D,I:Denise Pickering
DF:The Design Company

DESIGN AT THE ZOO
USA 1991
AD,D:Eric Rickabaugh
I:Michael Tennyson Smith DF:Rickabaugh Graphics
CL:The Art Directors Club of Cincinnati

AGENCY 6
USA 1991
CD:Charles Hively D:Tom Cleveland
DF:The Hively Agency CL:The Hively Agency

BRUSH STROKES IN FLIGHT
USA 1990
AD,D:Eric Rickabaugh DF:Rickabaugh Graphics
CL:Rickabaugh Graphics

ARA TOKYO SEATTLE HELSINKI MIAMI LOS A

IAAPA
USA 1991
D,I:Craig Hanna DF:Kevin Biles Design,Inc.
CL:Kevin Biles Design,Inc.

30/SIXTY DESIGN
USA
D:Henry Vizcarra,Jay Herrera

AXION DESIGN
USA 1991
CD:James McElheron AD,D,I:Eric Jon Read
DF:Axion Design,Inc.

SUPERSONIC
UK 1989
D:The Designers Republic
DF:The Designers Republic CL:The Designers Republic

TRADEMARK DESIGN
SOUTH AFRICA 1991
AD,D:Clive Gay DF:Trademark Design Limited

FRONT   BACK

trademark ('treid,mark) *n.* **1. a.** the name or other symbol used by a manufacturer or dealer to distinguish his products from those of competitors. **b. Registered Trademark.** one that is officially registered and legally protected. **2.** any distinctive sign or mark of the presence of a product or corporation. ~*vb.* (*tr.*) **3.** to label with a trademark. **4.** to register as a trademark.

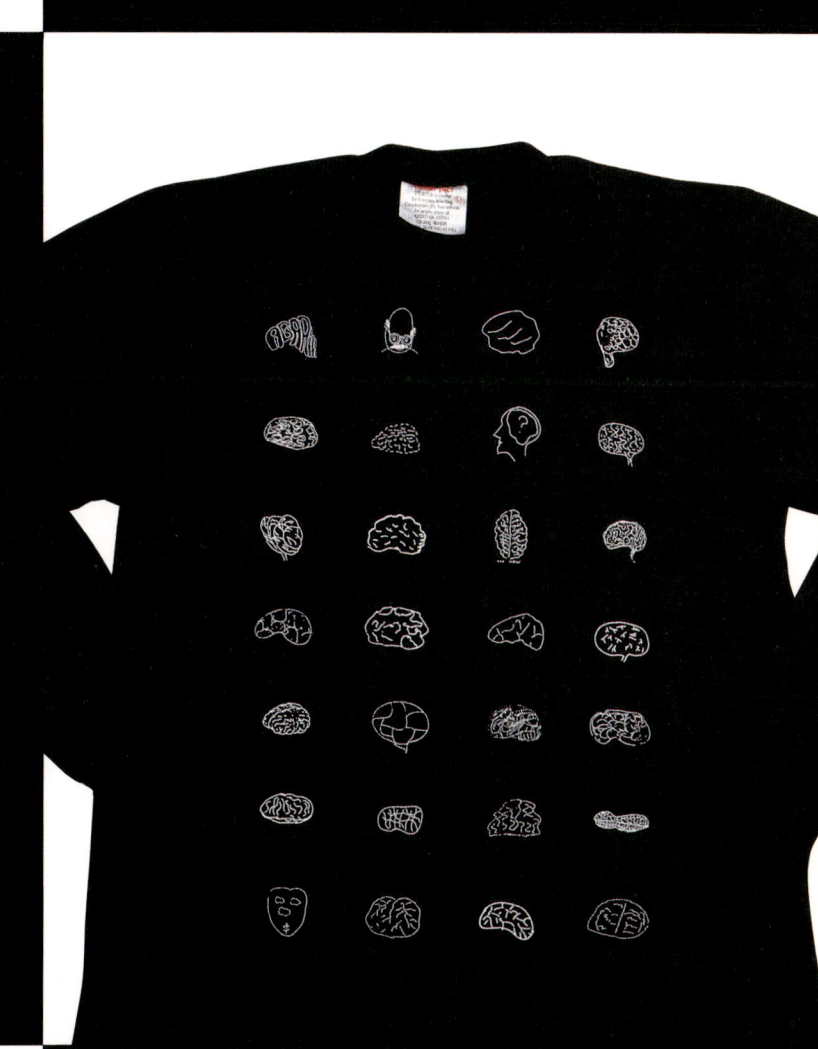

CAMP LEO
MACAU

BACK   FRONT

CAMP LEO
HONG KONG 1991
CD:Stefan Sagmeister AD:Peter Rae D,I:Mike Chan
DF:Leo Burnett Design Group CL:Leo Burnett

KYO SEATTLE HELSINKI MIAMI LOS ANGELES

ROGER AND ANGELICA ▲
JAPAN 1986
AD,D:Tadanori Yokoo
DF:Tadanori Yokoo Atelier CL:Art School

▼ ROGER AND ANGELICA
JAPAN 1986
AD,D:Tadanori Yokoo DF:Tadanori Yokoo Atelier
CL:Art School

NEW YORK MILANO DALLAS 146 AMSTERDA

NG KONG BOSTON PARIS SAN FRANCISCO OS

ADAM UND EVA
JAPAN 1983
AD,D,I:Tadanori Yokoo DF:Tadanori Yokoo Atelier
CL:Art School

TROUBLE ISSUE 4
UK 1987
D:David Crow CL:Trouble

JEANS
JAPAN 1989
AD:Takeshi Yamamoto

GUITAR AND WHITE SHOES
JAPAN 1989
AD:Takeshi Yamamoto

PHILADELPHIA LONDON SYDNEY 147 ATLAN

TTLE HELSINKI MIAMI LOS ANGELES HONG K

UNLIMITED VISIBILITY
USA 1991
D:Duane Meltzer P:Nick Barton
DF:Points of View CL:Points of View

AXION DESIGN
USA 1991
CD:Robert P.deVito AD,D,I:Eric Jon Read
DF:Axion Design,Inc.

GRAPHIC DESIGN USA
USA 1992
D:Louise Fili P:David Barry
DF:Louise Fili Ltd. CL:Louise Fili Ltd.

DICTIONAL ART
JAPAN 1992
AD,ARTIST:Noriyuki Tanaka
D:Ayako Yamazaki CL:Space Yui

RK 148 MILANO DALLAS AMSTERDAM PHILA

GOD SAVE THE QUEER
JAPAN 1992
D:Wataru Komachi(RAPE)

TROUBLE
UK 1991
D:David Crow CL:Trouble

HEADLIGHT
JAPAN 1989
AD:Takeshi Yamamoto

AI
UK 1983
D:Malcolm Garrett DF:Assorted Images
CL:Assorted Images

STEVE KEOUGH PHOTOGRAPHY ▲
AUSTRALIA 1991
AD,D:Barrie Tucker DF:Barrie Tucker Design Pty Ltd

▼ **ALPHA GRAPHIX TYPESETTER**
USA 1990
AD,D,I:Don Weller
DF:The Weller Institute for the Cure of Design,Inc.

FRONT　　　　　　　　　　　　　　　　　　　**BACK**

ART & DESIGN
USA 1992
D:Brad Boettcher
DF:Brad Boettcher Graphic Design CL:University of
Wisconsin-Stout-Department of Art & Design

HONBLUE MOVERS
USA 1991
CD,D,I:Keith Sasaki DF:Honblue Inc.

MICHAEL "MIKE" STANARD
TRADEMARK PARODY
USA 1991
AD,D:Michael Stanard DF:Michael Stanard,Inc.

THE END CLUB
JAPAN 1986
AD,D,I:Kenji Sakai DF:Simon Says Inc.

VAN HAYES DESIGN
USA 1988
D,I:Van Hayes DF:Van Hayes Design

TURQUOISE DESIGN
CANADA 1990
AD:Mark Timmings D,I:Daniel Lohnes
DF:Turquoise Design Inc.

POTTERING
JAPAN 1991
AD,D,I:Norikazu Machida DF:Machida Design

IS SAN FRANCISCO OSAKA NEW YORK MILAN

ROCKETS PASSING OVERHEAD
UK 1986
D:Steven Appleby DF:Assorted Images
CL:Assorted Images

ROBIN GHELERTER
USA 1988
AD,D,I:Robin Ghelerter CL:Robin Ghelerter

KAPOW
USA 1991
AD:Ken Hanson D:Cory DeWalt,Kathy Fabry
I:Jon Hargreaves DF:Hanson Graphic
CL:Delzer Lithograph Company

SPIRIT DANCER
USA 1992
D:Mohfei Geh DF:Mohfei Ger Fine Art
CL:Mohfei Geh Fine Art

SYDNEY 153 ATLANTA FERRARA TOKYO SEA

Q·LOGO IN AFRICA ▲
USA 1985
CD,D,I:Mike Quon DF:Mike Quon Design Office
CL:Mike Quon Design Office

▼ **D.N.T.FUNKY GINGER MIX**
JAPAN 1991
AD,D:Isamu Nakazawa DF:Hi·Hat Studio

FRANCISCO OSAKA NEW YORK MILANO DALL

FRONT

BACK

BIZARR SEX TRIO ▲
USA 1989
D,I:Paul B.Hirsch D:Martin Atkins CL:Invisible

▼ PIGFACE:GU
USA 1990
D,I:Francesca Sundsten D:Martin Atkins CL:Invisible

FRONT

BACK

Y ATLANTA FERRARA 155 TOKYO SEATTLE H

FRONT   BACK

TALKIN LOUD
UK 1991
AD,D:Ian Swift DF:Swifty Typographics
CL:Talkin Loud,Phonogram

INVISIBLE
USA 1991
D:Geoff Smyth

AMCA
UK 1991
D:JAFFA CL:A Man Called Adam

BIG APPLE SUBMISSION
UK 1989
D:The Designers Republic
DF:The Designers Republic CL:Submission Records

POP WILL EAT ITSELF:THIS IS THE HOUR
UK 1989
D:The Designers Republic
DF:The Designers Republic CL:Pop Will Eat Itself

BOY EUROPE
UK 1987
D:Malcolm Garrett DF:Assorted Images CL:Boy George

BOB MARLEY:EXODUS
USA 1990
D,I:Deborah Melian CL:The Island Trading Co.

92°F
UK 1991
D:The Designers Republic
DF:The Designers Republic CL:Pop Will Eat Itself

POP
UK 1991
D:The Designers Republic
DF:The Designers Republic CL:Pop Will Eat Itself

SUBSONIC 2:UNITY
UK 1991
D:The Designers Republic
DF:The Designers Republic CL:Unity Records

SUBSONIC 2:STEREOSPECTRUM
UK 1991
D:The Designers Republic
DF:The Designers Republic CL:Unity Records

NEW YORK MILANO DALLAS AMSTERDAM P

INCOGNITO!
UK 1991
AD,D:Ian Swift DF:Swifty Typographics
CL:Ricochet Management

**THE THREEPENNY OPERA:
DIE DREIGROSCHENOPER**
UK 1989
D:David Calderley CL:Decca Records

DANCING PEOPLE
USA 1989
D,I:Deborah Melian CL:Island Records,Inc.

BUZZCOCKS PRODUCT
UK 1989
D:Malcolm Garrett DF:Assorted Images CL:Buzzcocks

A TOKYO 159 SEATTLE HELSINKI MIAMI LOS

CHANGE IT ▲
USA 1991
CD:Joel Fuller AD,D:Tom Sterling I:Ralf Schuetz
DF:Pinkhaus Design Corp. CL:Sister Red

▼ **VOLANTE MAU MAU**
UK 1991
D:Mau Mau CL:Volante Record

BROTHER BEYOND BELIEF ▲
UK 1989
D:The Designers Republic
DF:The Designers Republic CL:EMI

▼ **KRUSH EXCLUSIVE AMERICAN FASHION**
UK 1988
D:The Designers Republic
DF:The Designers Republic CL:Fon Records

SAMPLE IT · LOOP IT · FUCK IT AND EAT IT! ▲
UK 1990
D:The Designers Republic
DF:The Designers Republic CL:Pop Will Eat Itself

▼ 22
UK 1991
D:The Designers Republic
DF:The Designers Republic CL:Chapter 22

HEAVEN 17
UK 1986
D:Malcolm Garrett DF:Assorted Images CL:Virgin

TRANSVISION VAMP
UK 1988
D:Malcolm Garrett,Jamie Reid
DF:Assorted Images CL:MCA

KOROVA MILK BAR
UK 1991
D:The Designers Republic DF:The Designers Republic

EMOTION LOTION
UK 1991
D:Helen Jones DF:Chameleon CL:TOP

...SAN FRANCISCO OSAKA NEW YORK MILA...

FRONT BACK

MADONNA ▲
USA 1991
D:Los Angeles T-shirt Museum

▼ ROLLING STONES:SEXDRIVE
UK 1991
D:David Crow, Garry Mouat CL:Sony Records

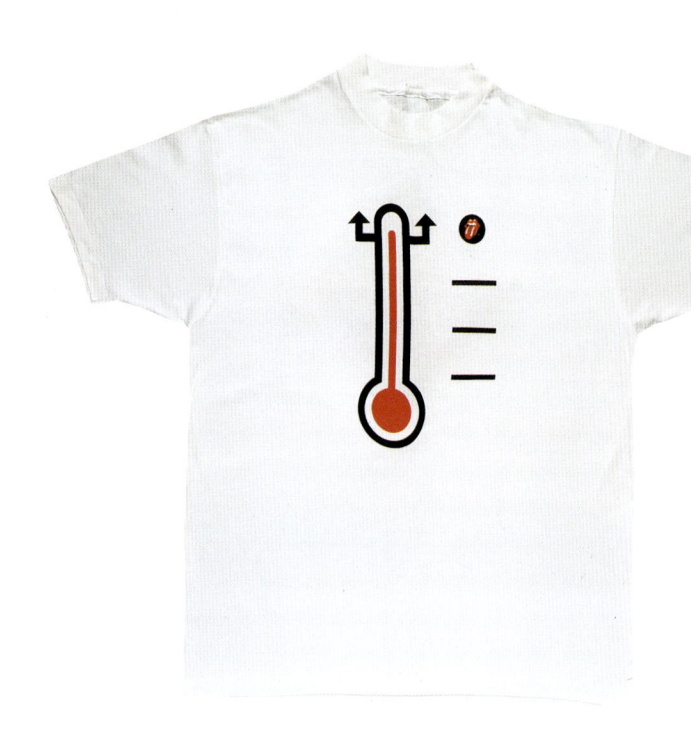

FRONT BACK

...EY ATLANTA 164 FERRARA TOKYO SEATTLE

DALLAS AMSTERDAM PHILADELPHIA LONDO

EUPHORIA
JAPAN
AD,D:Masaaki Hiromura PL,D:Seigo Kaneko
I:Toshiko Tsuchihashi CL:Power Box

THE WHO:THE KIDS ARE ALRIGHT TOUR 1989
USA 1989
D:Richard Evans
CL:The Who in Association with Winterland

QUICKSAND
USA 1991
AD,D,I:Melinda Beck

MILES
USA 1991
D,I:J.D.King CL:Downtown Music Gallery

ELSINKI MIAMI LOS ANGELES 165 HONG KON

ORIGINAL LOVE
JAPAN 1991
AD:Mitsuo Shindo D:Masako Saito P:Kenji Miura
DF:Contemporary Production CL:King Cobra

**FLIPPER'S GUITAR:
DOCTOR HEAD'S WORLD TOWER**
JAPAN 1991
AD:Mitsuo Shindo D:Sawako Nakajima
DF:Contemporary Production CL:Polystar Co.,Ltd.

BUZZCOCKS PRODUCT
UK 1989
D:Malcolm Garrett DF:Assorted Images CL:Buzzcocks

THROBBING GRISTLE
UK 1982
D:Malcolm Garrett DF:Assorted Images CL:Fetish

ISTERDAM PHILADELPHIA LONDON SYDNEY A

U2
USA 1991
D:Los Angeles T-Shirt Museum

PALE SAINTS "KINKY LOVE"
UK 1992
D:Vaughan Oliver CL:Rockin T

NIRVANA
USA 1991
D:Los Angeles T-Shirt Museum

SLOWDIVE "GREEN"
UK 1992
CL:Rockin T

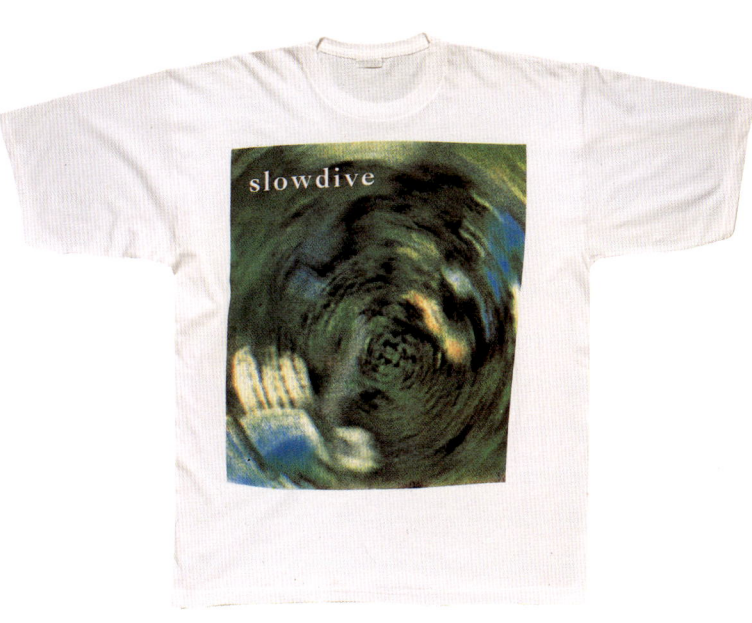

LOS ANGELES HONG KONG BOSTON 167 PARI

AKA NEW YORK MILANO DALLAS AMSTERDA

FOETUS
UK 1989
D:Malcolm Garrett,J.G.Thirlwell
DF:Assorted Images CL:Foetus Interruptus

RX:CHEMICAL REACTION
JAPAN 1991
AD:Yasutaka Kato D:Hideki Sawa
DF:Above Us Only Sky Studio CL:Ki/oon Sony Records

PM DAWN:OF THE HEART
USA 1991
D:Hilary Neidhart I:Tyler,Nappy Threads
CL:Island Records,Gee St.Records

FLYING MAU MAU
UK 1991
D:Mau Mau CL:Flying Records

TOKYO 168 SEATTLE HELSINKI MIAMI LOS A

PHILADELPHIA LONDON SYDNEY ATLANTA FE

FRONT　　　　　　　　　　　　　　　　　　　　　　　　BACK

PM DAWN:COMETOSE ▲
UK 1992
D:David Calderley CL:Gee Street Management

▼ **SIMPLE MINDS**
UK 1982
D:Malcolm Garrett DF:Assorted Images

FRONT　　　　　　　　　　　　　　　　　　　　　　　　BACK

GELES 169 HONG KONG BOSTON PARIS SAN

W YORK MILANO DALLAS AMSTERDAM PHILA

FOREVER RECORDS
JAPAN 1985-1989
AD,D:Hiroyuki Oichi I:Teruhiko Yumura
DF:Rock Lichtenstein & The Rock'n Roll Aids Production
CL:Forever Records Co.,Ltd.

VIOLENT FEMMES AUSTRALIAN TOUR
USA 1992
AD:Ken Hanson D:Kathy Fabry I:Jon Hargreaves
DF:Hanson Graphic CL:Violent Femmes

VIOLENT FEMMES CUBIST MOTIF
USA 1992
AD:Ken Hanson D:Kathy Fabry I:Jon Hargreaves
DF:Hanson Graphic CL:Violent Femmes

FRONT BACK

SEATTLE HELSINKI MIAMI 170 LOS ANGELES

LPHIA LONDON SYDNEY ATLANTA FERRARA T

DANCE ON THE CITY
JAPAN 1983
AD,D,I:Tadanori Yokoo DF:Tadanori Yokoo Atelier
CL:NKB Co.,Ltd.

SAGACHO
JAPAN 1991
AD,D,I:Tadanori Yokoo DF:Tadanori Yokoo Atelier
CL:Sagacho Exhibit Space

KENTUCKY SHAKESPEARE FESTIVAL
USA 1991
D,I:Ruth Wyatt D:Kevin Wyatt
DF:Bark Like a Dog Design

CELEBRATE INTERDEPENDENCE JULY 4TH
USA 1991
D,I:Mary Lynn Sheetz
DF:Mary Lynn Sheetz Graphics CL:Alterni-T's

NG KONG BOSTON PARIS 171 SAN FRANCISC

MILANO DALLAS AMSTERDAM PHILADELPHIA

FRONT

BACK

1989 COSMIC CROQUET SHIRT "ALICE" ▲
USA 1989
D,I:Ruth Wyatt,Kevin Wyatt
DF:Bark Like a Dog Design
CL:Afterimages Dance Company

▼ **BLUES FEST**
USA 1991
D,I:Mark Rattin D:Ernest Christmas
DF:Mr.Digital CL:Chicago Special Events

FRONT

BACK

HELSINKI 172 MIAMI LOS ANGELES HONG KONG

THE TENTH FESTIVAL OF ASIAN ARTS
HONG KONG 1985
AD,D:Kan Tai-Keung
DF:Kan Tai-Keung Design & Associates Ltd CL:Urban Council

KORYU ARK
JAPAN 1978
AD,D,I:Tadanori Yokoo DF:Tadanori Yokoo Atelier
CL:Koryu Ark Executive Committee

THE 3RD FESTIVAL OF ASIAN ARTS
HONG KONG 1978
AD,D:Kan Tai-Keung
DF:Kan Tai-Keung Design & Associates Ltd CL:Urban Council

TOKYO:FROM AND SPIRIT
JAPAN 1987
AD,D:Tadanori Yokoo DF:Tadanori Yokoo Atelier
CL:Walker Art Center Minneapolice

LEONARDO AND VENICE
USA 1992
AD,D,I:Milton Glaser DF:Milton Glaser Inc
CL:Eco Publicita and Marketing S.R.C.

ICLA '91
JAPAN 1991 AD,D:Masaaki Hiromura D(LOGO):Ikko Tanaka
D:Takafumi Kusagaya PL:Seigo Kaneko
CL:The ICLA '91 Congress Executive Committee

HOLLAND DANCE FESTIVAL
NETHERLANDS 1991
D:F.Lieshout DF:Total Design bv

92 CENTRAL PENNSYLVANIA FESTIVAL OF THE ARTS
USA 1992
AD,D,I:Lanny Sommese DF:Sommese Design
CL:Central Pennsylvania Festival of the Arts

CENTRAL PENNSYLVANIA FESTIVAL OF
THE ARTS '90
USA 1990
AD,D,I:Lanny Sommese DF:Sommese Design
CL:Central Pennsylvania Festival of the Arts

BLACK SQUIRREL
USA 1991
D,I:Eva Bice DF:Signum Design
CL:Kent State University

RAUMA BIENNALE BALTICUM 1992
FINLAND 1992
AD:Jari Silvennoinen CL:The Rauma Art Museum

DUKE CITY MARATHON 1991
USA 1991
AD,D,I:Rick Vaughn DF:Vaughn/Wedeen Creative

RUN LIKE THE DICKENS
USA 1990
D,I:Ruth Wyatt,Kevin Wyatt
DF:Good Design CL:Preservation Alliance

NORTH AMERICAN CHAMPIONSHIP SAILING REGATTA
USA 1987 AD,D:Liz Hecker DF:Liz Hecker Design
CL:St Francis Yacht Club

REGATTA
USA 1991
D:Kristin Sommese DF:Sommese Design
CL:SI Barash Regatta

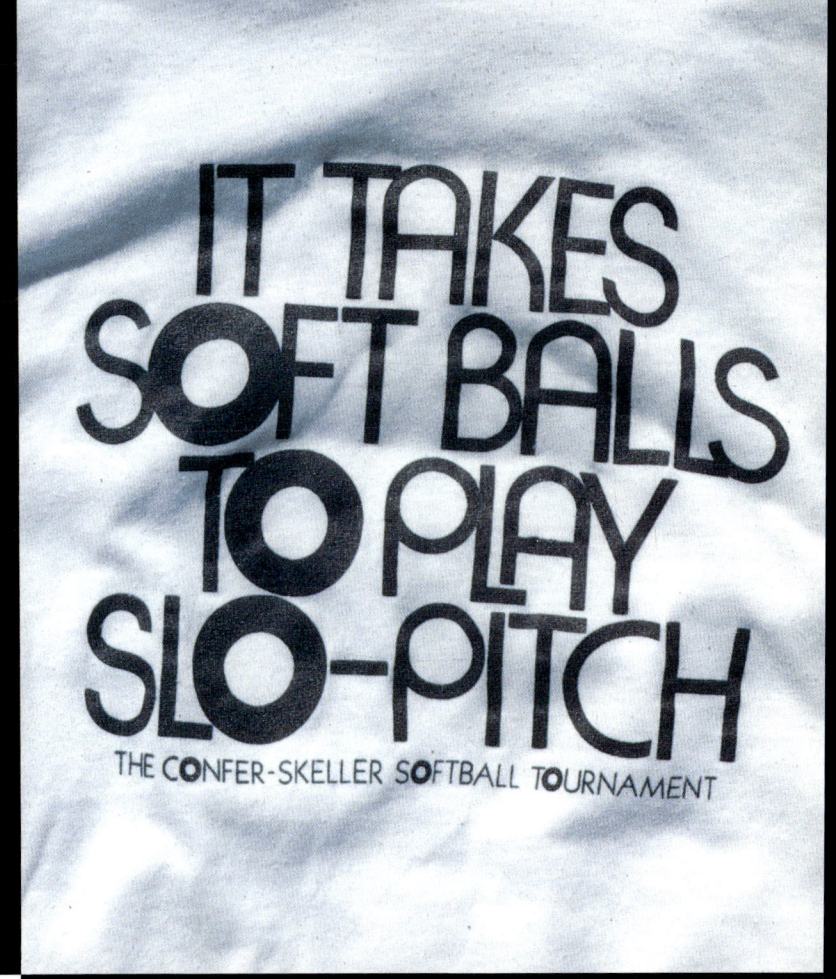

CENTRAL PENNSYLVANIA FESTIVAL OF THE ARTS 25TH YEAR
USA 1991 AD,D,I:Lanny Sommese DF:Sommese Design
CL:Central Pennsylvania Festival of the Arts

IT TAKES SOFTBALLS TO PLAY SLO-PITCH
USA 1990
AD,D,I:Lanny Sommese DF:Sommese Design
CL:Joel Confer,Rathskeller Softball Team

**ETCHELLS WORLD CHAMPIONSHIP
SAILING REGATTA**
USA 1991
AD,D:Liz Hecker I:Bob Dinetz
DF:Liz Hecker Design CL:San Francisco Yacht Club

REGENBOOG(RAINBOW)
NETHERLANDS 1989
AD,D:Marianne Vos I:Samenwerkende Ontwerpers
DF:Samenwerkende Ontwerpers

GEZOND 2000(HEALTH 2000)
NETHERLANDS 1989
AD,D:André Toet
I:Samenwerkende Ontwerpers
DF:Samenwerkende Ontwerpers CL:Museon

J24 US OPEN SAILING REGATTA
USA 1991
AD,D:Liz Hecker I:Sarah Waldron
DF:Liz Hecker Design CL:St Francis Yacht Club

A TOKYO SEATTLE HELSINKI MIAMI LOS ANG

RAIN CITY CLASSIC,1991
USA 1991
D,I:Barbara Edquist DF:Edquist Design
CL:Providence Foundation of Seattle

COMMOTION
CANADA 1986
CD:Lee Sackett D,I:Fernando Medina
DF:MLM CL:CN Pavillion-Expo 86-Vancouver Canada

COMUNE DI FERRARA-ITALY
ITALY 1990
AD,D,I:Fabio Adranno

1988 OLYMPIC YACHTING TRIALS REGATTA
USA 1988
AD,D:José Serrano I:Tracy Sabin
DF:Knoth & Meads CL:San Diego Yacht Club

SAKA NEW YORK MILANO 179 DALLAS AMST

A LONDON SYDNEY ATLANTA FERRARA TOKY

KEEP EVANSTON BEAUTIFUL CAMPAIGN
USA 1992
AD:Michael Stanard
D:Marc Fuhrman DF:Michael Stanard,Inc.
CL:Keep Evanston Beautiful,Inc.

OSTON PARIS 180 SAN FRANCISCO OSAKA NE

SEATTLE HELSINKI MIAMI LOS ANGELES HONG

WE'VE GOT THE BEAT
USA 1990
D:John Sayles DF:Sayles Graphic Design
CL:Drake University

FIREWORKS
USA 1990
AD:Ken Hanson D:Kathy Fabry I:Jon Hargreaves
DF:Hanson Graphic CL:First Wisconsin

NY ROAD RACE
USA 1990
CD,D:Gail Rigelhaupt CD:Harris Silver
DF:Rigelhaupt Design CL:NY Roadrunners Club

WILDLIFE 5K RUN/WALK
USA 1992
D,I:Cary Chow DF:RKS Design CL:Bikesport

YORK 181 MILANO DALLAS AMSTERDAM PH

N SYDNEY ATLANTA FERRARA TOKYO SEATT

FRONT BACK

1990 COSMIC CROQUET SHIRT "ROBOT" ▲
USA 1990
D,I:Ruth Wyatt,Kevin Wyatt
DF:Bark Like a Dog Design
CL:Afterimages Dance Company

▼ **1991 COSMIC CROQUET SHIRT "TWEEDLE"**
USA 1991
D,I:Ruth Wyatt,Kevin Wyatt
DF:Bark Like a Dog Design
CL:Afterimages Dance Company

FRONT BACK

ON PARIS SAN FRANCISCO 182 OSAKA NEW

HELSINKI MIAMI LOS ANGELES HONG KONG

FRONT BACK

JAZZ FEST ▲
USA 1991
D,I:Mark Rattin D:Ernest Christmas
DF:Mr.Digital CL:Chicago Special Events

▼ 50 MILE RACE SERIES
USA 1992
AD,D,I:Don Weller
DF:The Weller Institute for the Cure of Design,Inc.
CL:Industrial Supply Company

FRONT  BACK

RK MILANO DALLAS 183 AMSTERDAM PHILA

BACK

FRONT

SUNSPLASH
USA 1992
AD,D:Ken Hanson I:Jon Hargreaves
DF:Hanson Graphic CL:Niceman Merchandising,Inc.

FIREWORKS
USA 1989
AD:Ken Hanson D:Kathy Fabry I:Jon Hargreaves
DF:Hanson Graphic CL:First Wisconsin

JAZZ
USA 1989
D,I:Candace Kuss DF:Candace Kuss Design
CL:Charles Square

KI MIAMI LOS ANGELES HONG KONG BOSTO

JAZZ AND RIB FEST
USA 1991
AD,D:Mark Krumel DF:Rickabaugh Graphics
CL:City of Columbus,Department of Parks and Recreation

DALLAS AMSTERDAM PHILADELPHIA 185 LO

FORCEFIELD ▲
AUSTRALIA 1991
AD,D,I:Graham Rendoth DF:Reno Design Group
CL:New South Wales Board of Studies

▼ **PYMBLE LADIES COLLEGE**
AUSTRALIA 1990
AD:Raymond Bennett D,I:Pamela Sandberg
DF:Raymond Bennett Design Associates Pty Limited

MONTEREY CONFERENCE 1989
USA 1989
CD,D,I:Michael Dunlavey D:Heidi Tomlinson
DF:The Dunlavey Studio,Inc.
CL:California Council of
American Institute of Architects

MONTEREY CONFERENCE X
USA 1991
CD,I:Michael Dunlavey D:Heidi Tomlinson
I:Terry Green,Jack Paddon,Matt Holmes
DF:The Dunlavey Studio,Inc.
CL:California Council of
American Institute of Architects

MONTEREY CONFERENCE 1989
USA 1989
CD,D,I:Michael Dunlavey D:Heidi Tomlinson
DF:The Dunlavey Studio,Inc.
CL:California Council of
American Institute of Architects

SACRAMENTO COUNTY FAIR
USA 1992
CD:Michael Dunlavey D,I:Heidi Tomlinson
DF:The Dunlavey Studio,Inc.
CL:52nd District Agricultural Association

ARA TOKYO SEATTLE HELSINKI MIAMI LOS A

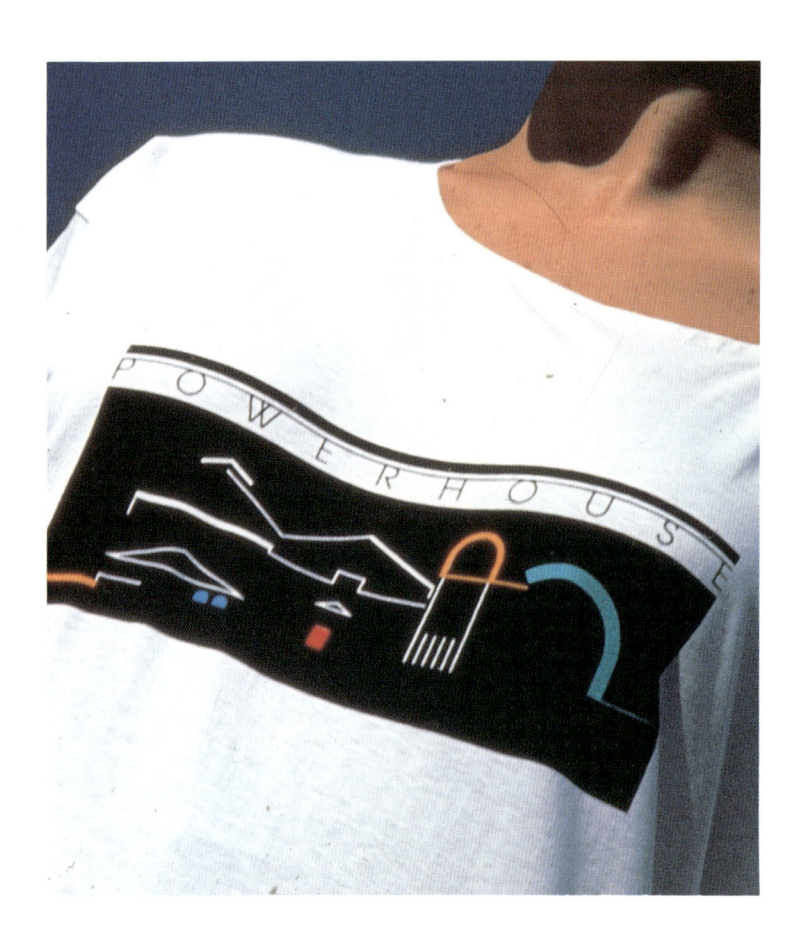

POWERHOUSE
AUSTRALIA 1986
CD:Garry Emery AD,D,I:Emery Vincent Associates
DF:Emery Vincent Associates
CL:Museum of Applied Arts and Sciences

DESIGN CAMP
USA 1988
AD:Daniel Olson,Charles S.Anderson
D:Daniel Olson,Kobe I:Daniel Olson
DF:Charles S.Anderson Design Company
CL:Aiga Minnesota

MCAD
USA 1989
AD:Charles S.Anderson,Daniel Olson
D:Daniel Olson,Charles S.Anderson
DF:Charles S.Anderson Design Company
CL:Minneapolis College of Art and Design

MUSEUM OF CONTEMPORARY ART, SAN DIEGO
USA 1992
AD:Kit Hinrichs D:Susan Tsuchiya
DF:Pentagram Design

CO OSAKA NEW YORK 188 MILANO DALLAS

THE BROOKLYN HOSPITAL CENTER
USA 1990
AD,D:Dean Morris DF:Stylism

WASHINGTON SOFTWARE ASSOCIATION
USA 1990
AD,D:Jack Anderson D,I:Julia LaPine
D:Lian Ng I:Brian O'Neill
DF:Hornall Anderson Design Works

**SACRAMENTO ZOO'S 65TH
BIRTHDAY CELEBRATION**
USA 1992
CD:Michael Dunlavey D:Kevin Yee I:Dave Stevenson
DF:The Dunlavey Studio,Inc. CL:Sacramento Zoo

BUENA VISTA COLLEGE
USA 1991
AD,D:John Sayles DF:Sayles Graphic Design

YO SEATTLE HELSINKI MIAMI LOS ANGELES

KEEP THE PRESSURE ON APARTHEID
　　　　　　　　　USA 1991
　　D:Clive Helfet CL:The Africa Fund

LONDON LIGHTHOUSE
　　　　　　　　　UK 1991
　　D:Sophie Herxheimer CL:London Lighthouse

AMNESTY INTERNATIONAL
USA 1991
D:Susi Oberhelman I:David Dias
DF:Eric Baker Design Assoc.Inc.

PLAY YOUR CARDS RIGHT
USA 1990
D:John Sayles DF:Sayles Graphic Design
CL:University of California,Berkeley

A NEW YORK MILANO DALLAS 190 AMSTERD

BE TRUE TO YOUR SCHOOL
USA 1991
D:Dave Holt,Michelle LaConto
DF:Hawthorne/Wolfe,Inc. CL:Old Bonhomme School

SAN ANTONIO PUBLIC LIBRARY
USA 1991
AD,D,I:Brad Lawton
DF:The Bradford Lawton Design Group

NUTURE NATURE
USA 1990
AD:Kathy Wilcoxin D,I:Steven Guarnaccia
DF:Studio Guarnaccia CL:Nature Conservancy

CENSORED-WORLD ISSUE
USA 1991
D:Los Angeles T-Shirt Museum

BLACK FASHION MUSEUM
USA 1992
AD,D:Takaaki Matsumoto AD:Michael McGinn
DF:M Plus M Incorporated CL:Fashion Institute of Technology

BIODIVERSITY AND LANDSCAPES
USA 1990
AD,D,I:Lanny Sommese DF:Sommese Design
CL:Conference at Penn State University

THE POOL
USA 1990
AD,D,I:Brad Lawton D,I:Jody Laney
DF:The Bradford Lawton Design Group CL:Rick Shaw

ASSOCIAZIONE CINOFILA CITTÀ DI FERRARA
ITALY 1989
AD,D:Graziano Uillani

BOSTON PARIS SAN FRANCISCO OSAKA NE

LOUIS KAHN
USA 1992
D,I:John Luckett P:Coastal Printworks,Inc.
CL:Museum of Contemporary Art

SMPS TEAM BUILDING
USA 1989
D,I:Toni Schowalter I:David Schowalter
DF:Schowalter 2 Design
CL:Society for Marketing Professional Seruices

BALLARD PRIDE
USA 1990
AD:Daniel Olson,Charles S.Anderson
D:Charles S.Anderson,Daniel Olson I:Randall Dahlk
DF:Charles S.Anderson Design Company
CL:Jerry French

MOCA MOCA MOCA
USA 1992
P:Coastal Printworks,Inc.
CL:Museum of Contemporary Art

PHIA LONDON 193 SYDNEY ATLANTA FERRA

HELSINKI MIAMI LOS ANGELES HONG KONG B

MOCA
USA 1992
P:Coastal Printworks,Inc.
CL:Museum of Contemporary Art

CORONA DEL MAR SCENIC FIVE-K
USA 1992
D,I:John Cosby P:Coastal Printworks,Inc.
CL:City of Newport Beach

THE PEOPLE MAKE THE EARTH
JAPAN 1979
AD,D:Tadanori Yokoo DF:Tadanori Yokoo Atelier
CL:Takamatsu Tax Office

WELLESLEY COLLEGE MUSEUM CENTENNIAL
USA 1990
AD,D:Karin Fickett,Anita Meyer
DF:plus design inc. CL:Wellesley College Museum

ANO DALLAS AMSTERDAM 194 PHILADELPHI

TON PARIS SAN FRANCISCO OSAKA NEW YOR

UKIYOE
UK 1991
DF:Gurtler+Hazell CL:British Museum

CND
UK 1991
D:Paul Aston CL:CND

WILD THING-DOLPHIN
UK 1992
D:Tony Jennings of Newart
CL:Green Peace

WILD THING-SEAL
UK 1992
D:Tony Jennings of Newart
CL:Green Peace

LONDON SYDNEY ATLANTA 195 FERRARA TO

MIAMI LOS ANGELES HONG KONG BOSTON

BEAR
UK 1992
D,I:Ian Wright CL:Lynx

ECOLOGY NOW
USA 1992
D:Los Angeles T-Shirt Museum

CND
UK 1990
D:Paul Aston CL:CND

MAKE LOVE NOT WAR
UK 1992
D:Paul Aston CL:CND

LLAS 196 AMSTERDAM PHILADELPHIA LOND

NATIONAL CONDOM WEEK
USA 1992
CD:Tommer Peterson AD,D,I:James Forkner
D:Dan Baker DF:Wilkins & Peterson
CL:Northwest AIDS Foundation

HOT SEX
UK 1992
D:Terrence Higgins Trust

PALAIS DE DANCE
UK 1991
D:Sophie Herxheimer CL:London Lighthouse

USE YOUR HEAD
UK 1992
D:Insight Designs

LOS ANGELES HONG KONG BOSTON PARIS SA

THE SHAM & THE SHAME
"WE SAW WHAT YOU DID!"
USA 1992
D:Craig Jones DF:Grand Slam Graphics
CL:Grand Slam Graphics

THE SHAM & THE SHAME
USA 1992
D:Craig Jones DF:Grand Slam Graphics
CL:Grand Slam Graphics

GIN LANE
UK 1991
D:G & H"After Hogarth" DF:Gurtler+Hazell
CL:British Museum

BRITISH INSTITUTE OF RADIOLOGY
UK 1991
D:Guy Hazell DF:Gurtler+Hazell

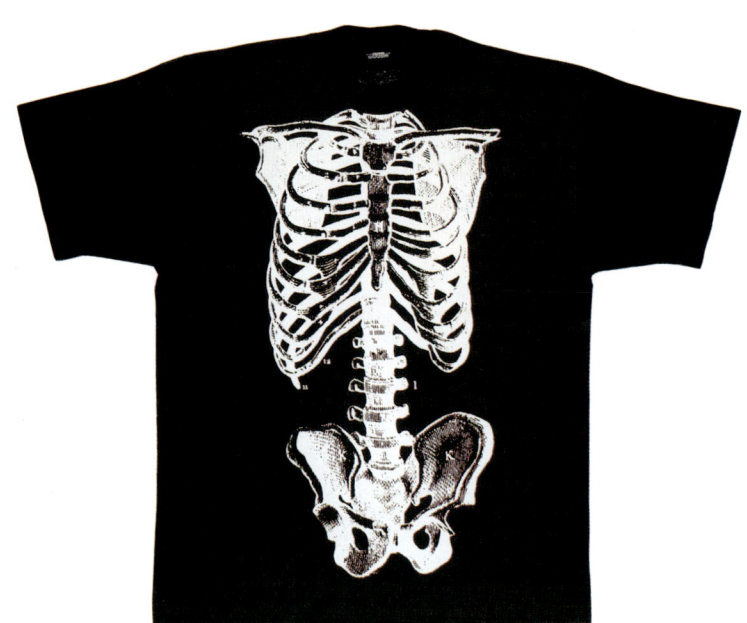

ISTERDAM PHILADELPHIA 198 LONDON SYD

SILENCE=DEATH
USA 1987
D:Silence=Death Project CL:Act Up

AFTER RODIN
UK 1992

HELP AMERICA'S HOMELESS
USA
D:Stan Bonnes

FOCUS AFRICA
CANADA 1991
AD,I:Malcolm Waddell D:Sandi King DF:Eskind Waddell
CL:African Medical and Research Foundation

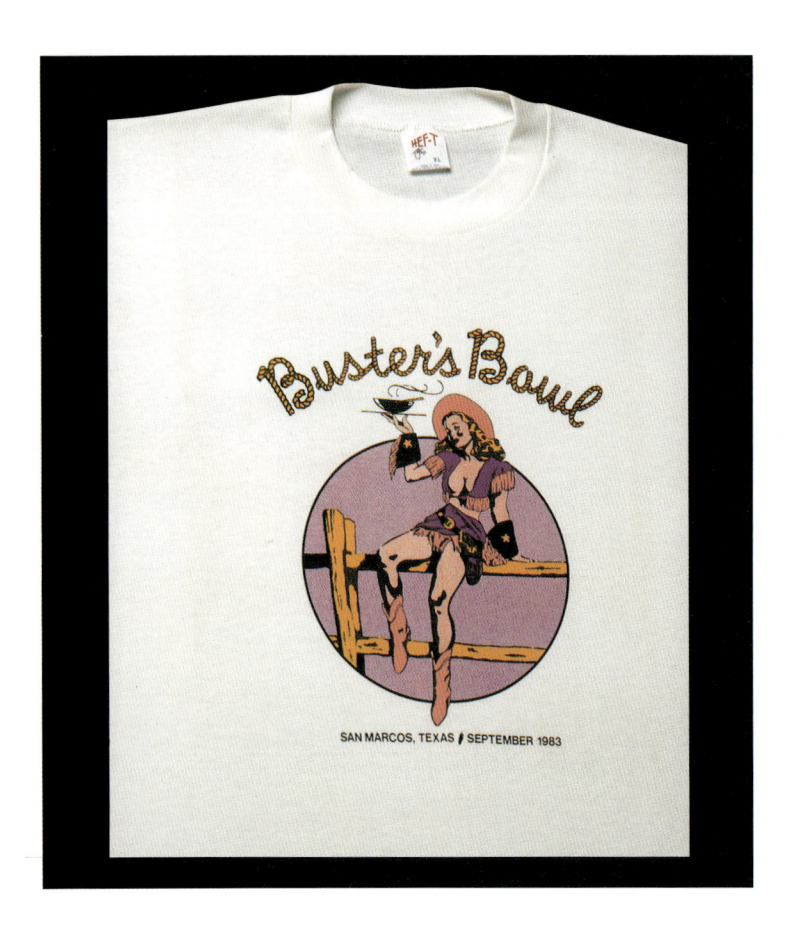

BUSTER'S BOWL
USA 1983
D,I:Van Hayes DF:Van Hayes Design CL:Buster Moore

BUSTER'S BOWL
USA 1984
D,I:Van Hayes DF:Van Hayes Design CL:Buster Moore

BUSTER'S BOWL
USA 1986
D,I:Van Hayes DF:Van Hayes Design CL:Buster Moore

BUSTER'S BOWL
USA 1991
D,I:Van Hayes DF:Van Hayes Design CL:Buster Moore

DADDY-O'S
USA 1989
CD,D:Michael Dunlavey DF:The Dunlavey Studio,Inc.

JIM DENNY'S HAMBURGERS
USA 1989
CD:Michael Dunlavey D:Heidi Tomlinson
DF:The Dunlavey Studio,Inc.

TANGO
USA 1990
CD:Michael Dunlavey D:Heidi Tomlinson
DF:The Dunlavey Studio,Inc.

FABULOUS FIFTIES CAFE
USA 1989
CD:Michael Dunlavey D:Heidi Tomlinson
DF:The Dunlavey Studio,Inc.

FRONT　　　　　　　　　　　　　　BACK

LOGO-MOTIVE
USA 1991
D:John Sayles DF:Sayles Graphic Design

HAMMER FILMWORKS
USA 1991
D,I:Rick Morris DF:Rick Morris Design
CL:Hammer Filmworks

COPY? WE DON'T NEEDED NO STINKIN' COPY!
USA 1991
D,I:William Homan DF:John Ryan Co. CL:John Ryan Co.

STRAIGHT NO CHASER
UK 1991
AD,D:Ian Swift I:Ian Wright
DF:Swifty

STRAIGHT NO CHASER
UK 1991
AD,D:Ian Swift I:Chris Long
DF:Swifty

VOUT-OROONIE 547
UK 1991
D:The Designers Republic
DF:The Designers Republic CL:The Leadmill

CLOCKWORK ORANGE
UK 1990
D:Malcolm Garrett DF:Assorted Images
CL:Royal Shakespeare Company

G BOSTON PARIS SAN FRANCISCO OSAKA NE

HAMMER COMPANY
USA 1991
D,I:Rick Morris DF:Rick Morris Design
CL:Hammer Filmworks

AERA
JAPAN 1990
AD,D:Tadanori Yokoo DF:Tadanori Yokoo Atelier
CL:Asahi Shinbun Publishing Company

PRANA
USA 1991
D,I:Lael Robertson DF:DBA Homefries
CL:Prana Investments

MENTOS
USA 1991
D,I:Dan Bittman I:Beverly Fox
DF:Design Team One,Inc. CL:Van Melle,Inc.

A LONDON SYDNEY ATLANTA 204 FERRARA

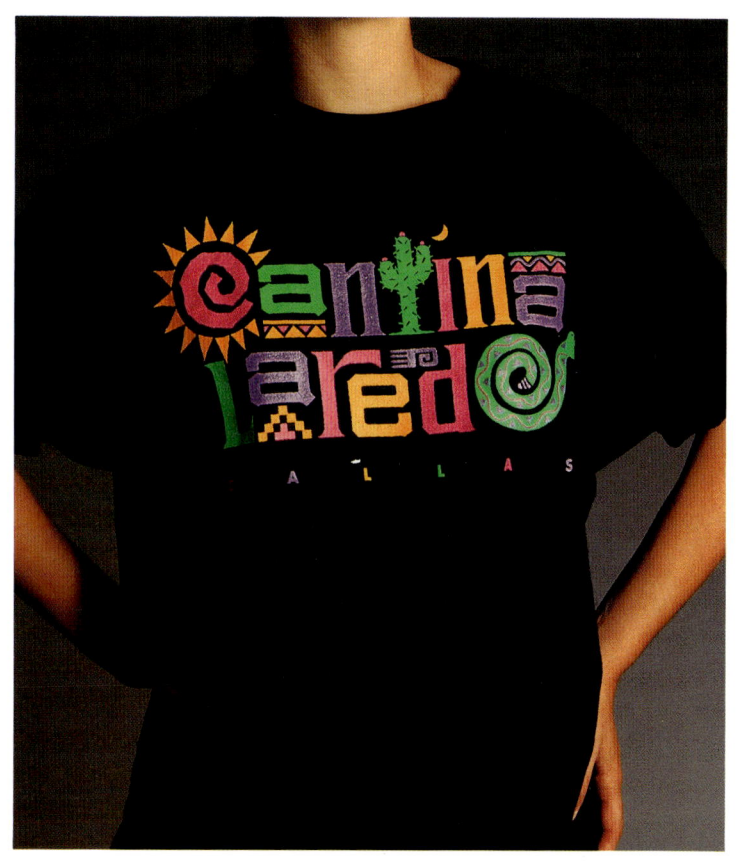

INTEL MATH COPROCESSOR
USA 1991
AD,D:Jack Anderson,Julia LaPine D:Heidi Hatlestad
I:Scott McDougall DF:Hornall Anderson Design Works
CI:Intel Corporation

SUMMER OUTING
USA 1991
AD,D,I:Marcia Romanuck I:Clip Art
DF:The Design Company
CL:Harodite Finishing Company

CANTINA LAREDO
USA 1991
AD,D,I:Pamela Chang DF:RBMM/The Richards Group
CL:Southwest Cafe Inc.

EXECUTIVE SURF CLUB
USA 1990
AD,D,I:Brad Lawton D,I:Jody Laney
DF:The Bradford Lawton Design Group

ITALIA
USA 1990
AD,D:Jack Anderson D,I:Julia LaPine
DF:Hornall Anderson Design Works

TREE SHIRT
UK 1989
AD:Andy Ewan D:Sarah Louis Allen
DF:The Yellow Pencil Company Limited
CL:The Yellow Pencil Company Limited

HOGAN'S MARKET
USA 1990
AD,D:Jack Anderson,Julia LaPine D:Denise Weir,Lian Ng
I:Larry Jost DF:Hornall Anderson Design Works
CL:Puget Sound Marketing Corporation

K2 ACTION PLUS,EURO PLUS,BASE PLUS
USA 1990
AD,D,I:Jack Anderson D,I:Jani Drewfs
D:Denise Weir,Julie Tanagi-Lock
DF:Hornall Anderson Design Works CL:K2 Corporation

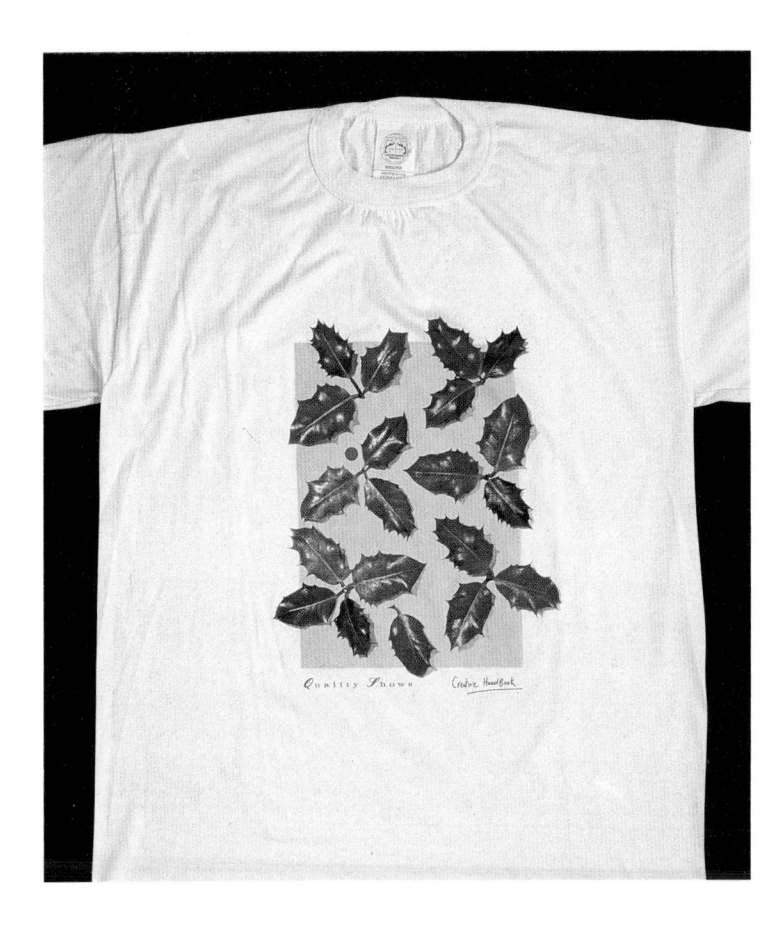

BOITE À GRAINS
CANADA 1990
AD:Mark Timmings D:Mario Godbout
DF:Turquoise Design Inc.

BOITE À GRAINS
CANADA 1990
AD:Mark Timmings D:Mario Godbout
DF:Turquoise Design Inc.

MADE IN WISCONSIN
USA 1990
AD:Ken Hanson D:Hanson Graphic I:Joe Sutter
DF:Hanson Graphic CL:First Wisconsin

WATER STREET SEAFOOD COMPANY
USA 1990
AD:Brad Lawton D,I:Jody Laney
DF:The Bradford Lawton Design Group

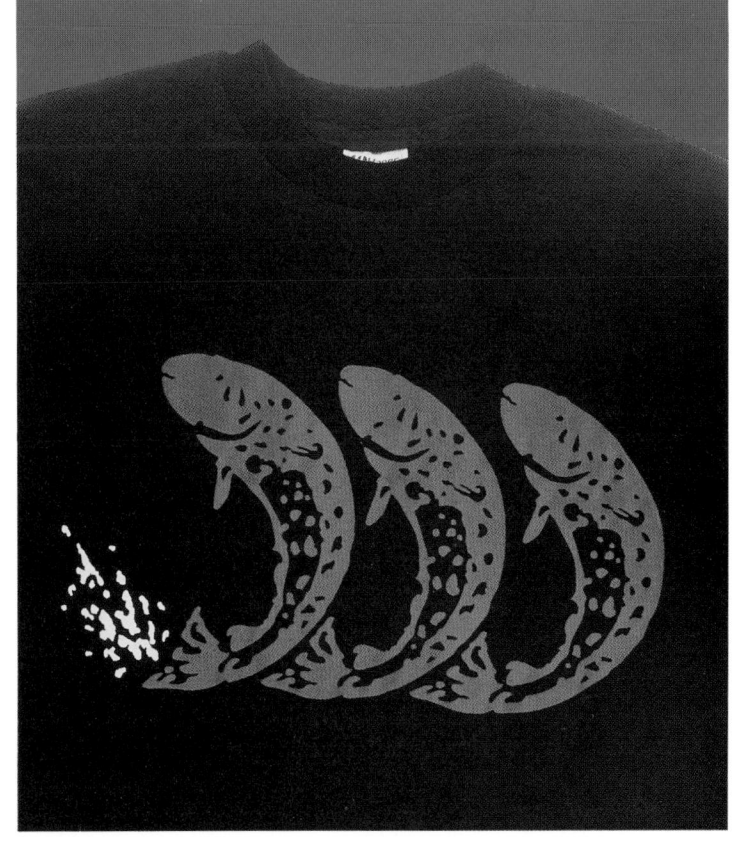

RORRIM:5
JAPAN 1987
AD,D,I:Tadanori Yokoo DF:Tadanori Yokoo Atelier
CL:Swatch Switzerland

FM802 "RICK DEES WEEKLY TOP40"
JAPAN 1991
AD:Keisuke Nagatomo D:Shigeki Kato
I:Seitaro Kuroda PR:Bow Co.,Ltd.

HOWARD'S CLASSIC DETAILING
USA 1992
P:Coastal Printworks Inc. CL:Howard's Detailing

PACIFIC DESIGN CENTER
USA 1992
AD:Kit Hinrichs D:Mark T.Selfe DF:Pentagram Design

DALLAS AMSTERDAM PHILADELPHIA LONDO

BOB ZOELL
USA 1990
D:Bob Zoell CL:City Restaurant

ZATOICHI
JAPAN 1992
AD,D:Yoshimi Takahashi CL:Pioneer LDC,Inc.

REEBOK '92 SPRING CAMPAIGN
JAPAN 1992
CD:Katsuyuki Nishizuka AD:Masayuki Shimizu
I:Wataru Hirose DF:Alfalfa Design Studio Co.,Ltd.
CL:Reebok Japan Inc.

GIGI'S PIZZA
USA 1991
AD,D,I:Pepe Orbein DF:Pepe Orbein+Associates

ELSINKI MIAMI LOS ANGELES 209 HONG KON

TIMEX
USA 1991
AD:Ken Hanson D:Claire Strykowski
DF:Hanson Graphic

BAY FM '90 SUMMER CAMPAIGN
JAPAN 1990
CD:Yukio Oka AD:Masayuki Shimizu D:Keiko Endo
DF:Alfalfa Design Studio Co.,Ltd. CL:Bay FM

GOLDSMITH,AGIO & COMPANY
USA 1990
AD:Charles S.Anderson,Daniel Olson
D:Daniel Olson,Charles S.Anderson
DF:Charles S.Anderson Design Company

OPLODE SYSTEM VISION
USA 1991
AD,D:Doug Akagi
I:John Hersey DF:Akagi Design CL:Oplode

GRINS RESTAURANT
USA 1990
D:Richard Whittington
DF:Whittington Design CL:Tom Wassenich

MAGAZINE
AUSTRALIA 1986
AD,D,I:Graham Rendoth DF:Reno Design Group
CL:The Magazine Partners

CLOCKWORK ORANGE
UK 1990
D:Malcolm Garrett DF:Assorted Images
CL:Royal Shakespeare Company

ECLECTIC
USA 1991
D,I:Rick Morris DF:Rick Morris Design
CL:Eclectic Camera,Grip & Electric

ACTIVE VOICE ▲
USA 1991
AD,D:Jack Anderson D:Julia LaPine,David Bates
DF:Hornall Anderson Design Works

▼ **LISTEN TO X-100FM**
USA 1991
CD,D:Rick Tharp DF:Tharp Did It
CL:Emmis Broadcasting

PHILADELPHIA LONDON SYDNEY ATLANTA F

ADMINISTAFF FALL CAMPAIGN
USA 1991
AD:Charles Hively D,I:Tom Cleveland
DF:The Hively Agency CL:Administaff

MABEL'S BEAUTY SHOT SOFTBALL
USA 1992
D:Leslie Voit Enander
DF:Leslie Voit Enander CL:Women's Softball Team

PORK BELLY FUTURES
USA 1991
D,I:Jennifer Bennett DF:Chicago Mercantile Exchange
CL:Chicago Mercantile Exchange

TOPPING THE CHARTS
USA 1991
AD:Eric Rickabaugh D:Tina Zientarski
I:Mike Linley DF:Rickabaugh Graphics
CL:Huntington Banks

GELES 213 HONG KONG BOSTON PARIS SAN

HAPPY VALLEY BREWERY
USA 1990
AD,D,I:Lanny Sommese
AD,D:Kristin Sommese DF:Sommese Design

REGISTA
ITALY 1991
AD,D:Nedda Bonini CL:Azzalli-Cinema Apollo-Ferrara

SANDRI SELLERIA FERRARA
ITALY 1991
AD:Ilde Ianigro

OSAMU GOODS STYLE
JAPAN 1992
D,I:Osamu Harada CL:Dusty Miller Co.Inc

PAUL KEATING'S QUOTES
AUSTRALIA 1992
AD,D:Graham Rendoth D:Morry Schwarz I:Mark Tremlett
DF:Reno Design Group CL:Bookman Press

REINDERS
NETHERLANDS 1989
AD,D:André Toet I:Samenwerkende Ontwerpers
DF:Samenwerkende Ontwerpers

RANDSTAD EMPLOYMENT AGENCY
NETHERLANDS 1990
D:Sacha Joseph DF:Total Design bv

CARMEN
AUSTRALIA 1990
CD:Garry Emery AD,D,I:Emery Vincent Associates
DF:Emery Vincent Associates
CL:Carmen Furniture Pty Ltd

SYDNEY ATLANTA FERRARA TOKYO SEATTL

GREEN STREET
USA 1991
AD,D:Stefan Sagmeister
DF:Sagmeister Graphics
CL:Tony Goldman

ROSES CAFE
USA 1991
AD,D,I:Stefan Sagmeister
DF:Sagmeister Graphics
CL:Tony Goldman

LUCKY'S RESTAURANT
USA 1991
AD,D:Stefan Sagmeister
I:Christoph Abbrederis
DF:Sagmeister Graphics
CL:Tony Goldman

STON PARIS 217 SAN FRANCISCO OSAKA NE

DANIEL WILLIAMS,ARCHITECT
USA 1991
AD:Joel Fuller D:Daniel Williams
I(LOGO):Anthony Russo DF:Pinkhaus Design Corp.

SUBMITORS' INDEX

A

A Man Called Adam 156
Abahouse International Company 60,90,91
Act Up 199
Akagi Design 210
Alfalfa Design Studio Co.,Ltd. 209,210
Antero Ferreira Design 103
Archaic Smile 21,22,25,64
Art Chantry 130
Assorted Images
54,149,153,157,159,163,166,168,169,203,211
Atelier Neu!! Inc. 48,56,71,74,77,86
Atelier Sab Co.,Ltd 44,61,90
Aussie Racing Apparel 136,137,138,139,140,141
Axion Design,Inc. 144,148

B

Bark Like a Dog Design 127,171,172,182
Barrie Tucker Design PTY Ltd. 150
Ba-tsu Co.,Ltd 45,48,74,75,86,97,105
Big Company 32,44
Body Rap 9,10,11,12,13,14,20,83
Bow Co.,Ltd. 208
Boy Bastiaens 113
Brad Boettcher Graphic Design 151
The Bradford Lawton Design Group
191,192,205,207
Bunkaya Zakkaten 20,62,63,64,65,66,67,80,81,83

C

Candace Kuss Design 184
Cane Haul Road,Ltd. 81
Chameleon 163
Charles S.Anderson Design Company
188,193,210
Chicago Mercantile Exchange 213
City Restaurant 209
Cizna Inc. 46,47,82,100
Clive Helfet 190
Club King Co. 36,37,40,41,42,45,53,86,89
CND 195,196
Coastal Printworks Inc.
91,100,101,124,193,194,208
Coconuts Company 78
Contemporary Production 166
Crazy Shirts,Inc. 126,131

D

David Calderley 159,169
David Crow 147;149,164
DBA Homefries 204
D.Brooks Design 8,15,17,21
Deborah Melian 157,159
Delor Design Group 127
The Design Company 143,205
Design Team One,Inc. 204
The Designers Republic
33,144,157,158,161,162,163,203

Designosaurus Rex 130
Dolphin Agencies 23,28,29,30,31
The Dunlavey Studio,Inc. 187,189,201
Dusty Miller Co.Inc 214

E

East Point Co.,Ltd. 112,115,117,121
Edquist Design 179
The Ellebis,Ltd. 62
Emery Vincent Associates 135,188,216
Eric Baker Design 190
Eskind Waddell 199

F

Flying Records Ltd 160,168

G

Galerie de Pop Co.,Ltd 76,91
Geoff Smyth 156
Good Design 176
Gotcha Sportswear 126,127
Grand Slam Graphics 198
Graziano Uillani 179,192
Gulter + Hazell 21,24,34,35,195,198

H

Hanson Graphic 153,170,181,184,207,210
Hawthorne/Wolfe,Inc. 191
Hiromura Design Office Inc. 165,174
Hirosuke Ueno 87
The Hively Agency 143,213
Honblue Inc. 151
Hornall Anderson Design Works
189,205,206,212

I

Ian Wright 196,203
Invisible 155
Isamu Nakazawa 154
Island Records 168

J

Jari Silvennoinen 176
J.D.King. 165
Joe Boxer Corp. 37,45,80
Joe Casaly-Hayford 30,43
John Richmond 23,35,43,44
John Ryan Co. 202
Joi'x Corporation 84
Joji Yano 57,75,77,92,94,95

K

Kan Tai-keung Design&Associates Ltd 173
Kansai Company 51,88,89
Katz Wheeler Design Group 142
Ken Brown Designs 15,16,81
Kenji Sakai 152
Kevin Biles Design Inc. 144

L

Lemon Co.,Ltd. 27,37,38,50,56,
58,59,60,61,77,84
Leo Burnett Ltd 145

Leslie voit Enander 213
Liz Hecker Design 177,178
London Lighthouse 190,197
Los Angeles T-shirt Museum 23,91,109,110,164,167,191,196
Louise Fili Ltd. 148

M
Machida Design 152
Mary Lynn Sheetz Graphics 171
Melinda Beck 165
Melrose Co.,Ltd 79,93
Men's Bigi Co.,Ltd. 79
Merchandising Management 98,99,100,167,195
Michael Stanard,Inc. 126,128,129,151,180
Mike Quon Design Office 154
Milk Inc. 69
Milton Glaser Inc. 174
Mohfei Geh Fine art 153
Morla Design,Inc. 102
Mossimo Inc. 122
M Plus M Incorporated 192
Mr.Digital 172,183

N
Nedda Bonini 214
Nike Inc. 108,110,111
Nine Too Zero 38,39
Noriyuki Tanaka 148

O
Ozone Community Co.,Ltd 18,19,22,26,27,62,63,68

P
Pacific Eyes & T's 127
Pentagram Design 96,188,208
Pepe Orbein + Associates 209
Person's Co.,Ltd. 50,73,84,93,95
The Planet Plan,Inc. 40,41,51,52,53,56,92
plus design inc. 194
Pinkhaus Design Corp. 160,218
Point of View 148
Powder 70,72,73

R
Rakuen Co.,Ltd 92
Raymond Bennett Design Associates Ltd. 186
RBMM/The Richards Group 205
Red or Dead 43,66
Reno Design Group 103,186,211,215
Richado Evans 165
Richard W.Salzman Artist representative 82
Rick Morris Design 202,204,211
Rickabaugh Graphics 143,185,213
Rigelhaupt Design 86,181
RKS Design 181
RNA Inc. 22,81,89
Rob Art,Inc. 126

Robin Ghelerter 153
Rock Lichtenstein& The Rock'n Roll Aids Production 170

S
Sabin Design 131,132,133,134,179
Sachico Ito/Sugar Inc 79
Sagmeister Graphics 217
Samenwerkende Ontwerpers 178,215
Sayles Graphics Design 181,189,190,202
Schowalter2 Design 193
Scoop Inc. 71,83
Seilin&Co. 54,55,57,76,95
Shobi Corporation 209
Signum Design 176
Skip Bolen Studio 60,75,87,97
Sommese Design 174,175,177,192,214
St.Evance Co.,Ltd 57,79,82
Stan Bonnes 199
Strange Attractions 34
Studio Guarnaccia 191
Stussy Incorporated 123
Stylism 189
Super Planning Co.,Ltd 27,85,92
Swifty Typographics 42,84,156,159,203

T
Tadanori Yokoo 24,36,146,147,171,173,194,204,208
Takeshi Yamamoto 147,149
The Terrence Higging Trust 197,199
Tharp Did It 212
Thirty-Three 33,36,43,48,49,50,51,61
Tokyo Can Co.Ltd 70,71
Total Design 174,215
Trademark Design Pty Ltd 145
Triom Design 179
Turquoise Design Inc. 152,207

U
United Agency K.K. 97,104,106,107
Urban Image 125

V
Van Hayes Design 152,200
Vaughn/Wedeen Creative 176

W
Wataru Komachi 149
The Weller Institute for the Cure Design,Inc. 150,183
Whittington Design 211
Wilkins&Peterson 197
World Sports Plaza 108,109,110,112,113,114,115,116,117,118,119,120,121,123

Y
Yasutaka Kato 168
The Yellow Pencil Company Limited 206

Z
Zonk Inc. 131

ART DIRECTOR
Kazuo Abe

DESIGNERS
Kazuo Abe
Kimiko Ishiwatari
Shinji Ikenoue

EDITORS
Toru Hachiga
Shinichi Kadota

ASSISTANT EDITOR
Minako Hakomori

PHOTOGRAPHERS
Kuniharu Fujimoto (ToKyo)
Andrew Cameron (London)
Rick Oyama (Los Angeles)

COORDINATORS
Sarah Phillips (London)
Roland Gebhardt Design (New York)
Intertrend (Los Angeles)

ENGLISH TRANSLATOR
Write Away Co.,Ltd.

THANKS TO
Takafumi Maeda (Cover C.G.work)

PUBLISHER
Shingo Miyoshi

1992年10月4日 初版第1版発行

発行所
ピエ ブックス
170 東京都豊島区駒込 4-14-6-407
TEL 03-3949-5010 FAX 03-3949-5650

製版,印刷,製本
弘陽印刷
116 東京都荒川区日暮里 4-8-12
TEL 03-3802-1221

© 1992 P·I·E BOOKS
Printed in Japan

本書の収録内容の無断転載、複写、引用等を禁じます。
落丁・乱丁はお取り替え致します。

ISBN4-938586-33-9 C3070 P16000E

REQUEST FOR SUBMISSIONS

作品提供のお願い

P·I·E Books, as always, has several new and ambitious graphic book projects in the works which will introduce a variety of superior designs from Japan and abroad. Currently we are planning the collection series detailed below. If you have any graphics which you consider worthy for submission to these publications, please fill in the necessary information on the inserted questionnaire postcard and forward it to us. You will receive a notice when the relevant project goes into production.

ピエ・ブックスでは、今後も新しいタイプのグラフィック書籍の出版を目指すとともに、国内外の優れたデザインを幅広く紹介していきたいと考えております。今後の刊行予定として下記のコレクション・シリーズを企画しておりますので、作品提供していただける企画がございましたら挟み込みのアンケートハガキに必要事項を記入の上お送り下さい。企画が近づきましたらそのつど案内書をお送りいたします。

A. POSTCARD GRAPHICS
A collection of various types of postcards including product advertising, direct mailers, invitations to events such as parties and fashion shows as well as birthday cards and seasonal greetings. In short all sorts of cards except the letter type which are mailed in envelopes.

A. ポストカード・グラフィックス
各シーズンのグリーティングカードをはじめとして、商品広告ＤＭ、パーティーやコレクション等のイベントのお知らせ、バースデイカードなど封書タイプを除く様々なポストカードをコレクションします。

B. ADVERTISING GREETING CARDS
A collection of letter-style direct mailers including sales promotional sheets, invitations to events such as exhibitions, parties and weddings. Some of these are quite simple, some have unusual shapes or dimensions (limited to cards inserted in envelopes).

B. アドバタイジング・グリーティングカード
販促用のＤＭ、展示会・イベントの案内状やパーティや結婚式などの招待状など、プレーンなものから形状の変わったもの・立体になったものまで封書タイプのＤＭをコレクションします。（封書タイプのものに限ります）

C. BROCHURE & PAMPHLET COLLECTION
A collection of brochures and pamphlets categorized according to the business of the client company. Includes sales promotional pamphlets, product catalogues, corporate image brochures gallery exhibitions, special events, annual reports and company profiles from all sorts of businesses.

C. ブローシュア＆パンフレット・コレクション
販促用パンフレット、商品カタログ、イメージ・カタログ、ギャラリーや展示会・イベントのパンフレット、アニュアル・リポート、会社案内など様々な業種のブローシュアやパンフレットを業種別にコレクションします。

D. POSTER GRAPHICS
A collection of posters, classified according to the business of the client. Fashion, department stores, automotive, food, home appliances and almost any sort of poster you might see on streets. Invitational posters for art exhibitions, concerts and plays as well as regional posters which will be seen for the first time outside of the local area where they were published.

D. ポスター・グラフィックス
ファッション、デパート、車、食品、家電など街角を飾る広告ポスター、美術展、コンサート、演劇などのイベント案内ポスター、見る機会の少ない地方のポスターなどを業種別にコレクションします。

E. BOOK COVER AND EDITORIAL DESIGNS
Editorial and cover designs for various types of books and magazines. Includes all sorts of magazines, books, comics and other visual publications.

E. ブックカバー＆エディトリアル・デザイン
雑誌、単行本、ヴィジュアル書、コミックなど様々なタイプの書籍・雑誌のエディトリアル・デザイン、カバー・デザインを紹介します。

F. CORPORATE IMAGE LOGO DESIGNS
A collection of C.I. materials mainly symbols and logos for corporations of all sorts, classified according to the type of business. In some cases, development samples and trial comps as well as the final designs are included. Includes logos for magazines and various products.

F. コーポレイト・イメージ・ロゴマーク・デザイン
企業やショップのシンボルマーク・ロゴマークを中心に幅広い業種にわたり分類しコレクションします。マークのみではなく展開例としてのアプリケーションも数多く紹介し、その他、雑誌や商品などの様々なロゴマークもコレクションします。

G. BUSINESS CARD AND LETTERHEAD GRAPHICS
A collection of cards such as the business cards of corporations and individuals as well as shopping cards for restaurants and boutiques, membership cards and various prepaid cards. This collection centers on business cards, letterheads and shopping cards of superior design.

G. ビジネスカード＆レターヘッド・グラフィックス
様々な企業や個人の名刺、レストランやブティックのショップカード、会員カード、プリペイドカードなど、デザイン的に優れたカードを名刺・ショップカードを中心にコレクション。またカードのみでなくレターヘッドも紹介します。

H. CALENDAR GRAPHICS
A collection of visually interesting calendars. We do not take into account the form of the calendar, i.e. wall hanging-type or note-type or desktop-type etc. So that the calendars represent the widest range of possibilities.

H. カレンダー・グラフィックス
ヴィジュアル的に優れたカレンダーをコレクションします。壁掛けタイプ、ノートタイプ、ダイアリー、日めくりタイプ、卓上タイプなど形状にはこだわらず幅広い分野の様々なタイプのカレンダーを紹介します。

I. PACKAGE AND WRAPPING GRAPHICS
A collection of packaging and wrapping materials of superior design from Japan and abroad. Includes related accessories such as labels and ribbons and almost anything else that comes under the heading of containing, protecting and decorating things.

I. パッケージ＆ラッピング・グラフィックス
商品そのもののパッケージデザインはもちろん、いろいろな物を包む、保護する、飾るというコンセプトで国内外の優れたパッケージ、ケース、ラッピング・デザイン及びラベル、リボンなどの付属アクセサリー類を幅広く紹介します。

DEMANDE DE SOUMISSIONS

AUFFORDERUNG ZU MITARBEIT

Comme toujours, P·I·E Books a dans ses ateliers plusieurs projets de livres graphiques neufs et ambitieux qui introduiront une gamme de modèles supérieurs en provenance du Japon et de l'étranger. Nous prévoyons en ce moment la série de collections détaillée cidessous. Si vous êtes en possession d'un graphique que vous jugez digne de soumettre à ces publications, nous vous prions de remplir les informations nécessaires sur l'étiquette à renvoyer située à la carte postale questionnaire insérée et de nous la faire parvenir. Vous recevrez un avis lorsque le projet correspondant passera à la production.

Wie immer hat P·I·E Books einige neue anspruchsvolle Grafikbücher in Arbeit, die eine Vielzahl von hervorragenden Designs aus Japan und anderen Ländern vorstellen werden. Momentan planen wir eine Serie mit den nachfolgend aufgeführten Themen. Wenn Sie grafische Darstellungen besitzen, von denen Sie meinen, daß sie in diese Veröffentlichung aufgenommen werden könnten, geben Sie uns bitte die nötigen Informationen auf der entsprechenden Antwortseite am füllen Sie die beigelegte Antwortkarte aus und schicken Sie sie an uns. Wir werden Sie benachrichtigen, wenn das entsprechende Projekt in Arbeit geht.

A. Graphiques pour cartes postales
Une collection de divers types de cartes postales, y compris la publicité de produits, l'adressage direct, des invitations à des événements tels que soirées et défilés de mode, ainsi que des cartes d'anniversaire et des voeux de saison. En bref, toutes sortes de cartes, à part le type lettre qui sera envoyé dans des enveloppes.

B. Cartes de voeux publicitaires
Une collection d'adressages directs style lettre y compris des feuilles de promotion de ventes, des invitations à des événements tels qu'expositions, soirées et mariages. Certaines d'entre elles sont très simples, d'autres ont des formes ou dimensions inhabituelles (limitées aux cartes insérées dans des enveloppes).

C. Collection de brochures et de pamphlets
Une collection de brochures et de pamphlets triées en fonction des affaires de la société client. Comprend des pamphlets de promotion des ventes, des catalogues de produits, des brochures sur l'image de la société, des expositions de galerie, des événements spéciaux, des compte-rendus annuels et des profils de sociétés de toutes sortes d'affaires.

D. Graphiques sur affiche
Une collection d'affiches, classées en fonction du secteur d'affaires du client. La mode, les grands magasins, l'automobile, l'alimentation, les appareils électro-ménagers et presque tous les types d'affiche que vous pouvez voir dans les rues. Des affiches invitant à des expositions d'art, des concerts et des pièces ainsi que des affiches régionales qui seront vues pour la première fois en dehors de la région où elles ont été éditées.

E. Designs de couverture de livre et d'éditorial
Des designs de livre et d'éditorial de divers types de livres et magazines. Comprend toutes sortes de magazines, livres, bandes dessinées et autres publications visuelles.

F. Designs de logo d'image de société
Une collection de matériaux d'image de société, principalement des symboles et des logos pour sociétés de toutes sortes ; classés en fonction du type d'affaires. Dans certains cas, sont inclus des échantillons de développement et également des compositions d'essai ainsi que les designs finaux. Comprend des logos pour magazines et divers produits.

G. Graphiques pour en-têtes et cartes de visite
Une collection de cartes telles que les cartes de visite de sociétés et d'individus ainsi que les cartes de fidélité de restaurants et de boutiques, les cartes de membre et diverses cartes payées à l'avance. Cette collection se concentre sur les cartes de visite, les en-têtes et les cartes de fidélité d'une qualité supérieure.

H. Graphiques pour calendrier
Une collection de calendriers visuellement intéressants. Nous ne tenons pas compte de la forme du calendrier, c.-à-d., type à accrocher au mur, type carnet ou type bureau, etc. de telle sorte que les calendriers représentent la gamme de possibilités la plus large.

I. Graphiques pour emballage et paquetage
Une collection de matériaux d'emballage et de paquetage de qualité supérieure en provenance du Japon et de l'étranger. Comprend des accessoires en relation tels qu'étiquettes et rubans, et presque tout ce qui est destiné à contenir, protéger et décorer des choses.

A. Postkarten-Grafik
Zusammenstellung verschiedener Postkartenarten, und zwar für Produktwerbung, Direkt Mailing, Einladungen zu Parties und Modenschauen sowie Geburtstagskarten und Karten zu verschiedenen Jahreszeiten. Also alle Arten von Karten, ausgenommen Briefkarten.

B. Werbe-Grußkarten
Zusammenstellung briefähnlicher Direkt-Mailings, wie z.B. verkaufsfördernde Texte, Einladungen zu Anlässen wie Ausstellungen, Parties oder Hochzeiten. Einige von ihnen sind recht einfach gemacht, andere fallen durch ungewöhnliches Aussehen oder Größe auf (Karten dürfen Umschlaggröße nicht überschreiten).

C. Zusammenstellung von Broschüren und Druckschriften
Diese Zusammenstellung von Broschüren und Druckschriften ist nach den Tätigkeiten der Kundenfirmen geordnet. Sie beinhaltet verkaufsfördernde Broschüren, Produktkataloge, Corporate-Image-Broschüren, Galerieausstellungen, besondere Veranstaltungen und Firmenprofile für alle Arten von Unternehmen.

D. Postergrafik
Eine Zusammenstellung von Postern, die nach dem Geschäftsgebiet des Kunden geordnet sind. Mode Kaufhäuser, Kraftfahrzeuge, Nahrungsmittel, Haushaltsgeräte und fast jede Art von Postern, die auf der Straße zu sehen sind. Einladungsposter für Kunstausstellungen, Konzerte und Theaterstücke ebenso wie Poster mit regionalen Themen, die zum ersten Mal außerhalb des Gebietes, in dem sie aufgehängt wurden, zu sehen sein werden.

E. Bucheinbände und redaktionelles Design
Bucheinbände und redaktionelles Design für verschiedenste Buch- und Zeitschriftentypen. Dies schließt alle Arten von Zeitschriften, Büchern, Comics und anderen visuellen Publikationen ein.

F. Corporate-Image-Logo-Design
Dies ist eine Zusammenstellung von C.I.-Material, und zwar hauptsächlich von Symbolen und Logos für Firmen aller Art, nach Geschäftsgebieten geordnet. In manchen Fällen sind die Arbeiten der Entwicklungsphase und Probeexemplare ebenso miteinbezogen wie das endgültige Design. Logos für Zeitschriften und andere Produkte sind miteingeschlossen.

G. Visitenkarten und Briefkopt-Grafik
Dies ist eine Zusammenstellung verschiedener Visitenkarten, z.B. für Firmen und Einzelpersonen, Kreditkarten für Restaurants und Boutiquen, Mitgliedskarten und Vorverkaufskarten. Diese Sammlung konzentriert sich vor allem auf geschäftliche Karten, Briefköpfe und Geschäftseigene Kreditkarten mit herausragendem Design.

H. Kalendergrafik
Eine Zusammenstellung von optisch interessanten Kalendern. Es ist für uns dabei unwichtig, ob es sich um die Form des Wandkalenders, Tischkalenders oder Notizbuchkalenders handelt, sodaß die größtmögliche Vielfalt an Kalendern gezeigt werden kann.

I. Grafik auf Verpackungen und Verpackungsmaterial
Eine Zusammenstellung von Grafik auf Verpackungen und Verpackungsmaterial mit herausragendem Design aus Japan und anderen Ländern. Dazugehörige Accessoires wie Etiketten und Bänder sind eingeschlossen, ebenso wie fast alles, was als Behälter für Produkte dienen kann, sie ziert oder schützt.